NEW ACCENTS

General Editor: TERENCE HAWKES

English and Englishness

9

IN THE SAME SERIES

English and Englishness

BRIAN DOYLE

R

ROUTLEDGE

London and New York

First published in 1989 by
Routledge
11 New Fetter Lane, London EC4P 4EE
29 West 35th Street, New York, NY 10001

© 1989 Brian Doyle

Photoset by Rowland Phototypesetting Ltd
Bury St Edmunds, Suffolk
Printed in Great Britain by
The Guernsey Press Co. Ltd, Guernsey, Channel Islands

British Library Cataloguing in Publication Data

Doyle, Brian, 1943–
    English and Englishness.— (New accents).
    1. Education. Curriculum subjects.
    English language
    I. Title   II. Series
    420'.7

ISBN 0-415-00981-2
    0-415-00982-0 Pbk

Library of Congress Cataloging in Publication Data

Doyle, Brian
    English and Englishness/Brian Doyle.
        p. cm.— (New accents)
    Bibliography: p.
    Includes index.
    1. English literature—Study and teaching.   2. English literature—
    Social aspects.   3. England—Popular culture.   4. Literature and
    society—England.   I. Title   II. Title: English and Englishness.
    III. Series: New accents (Routledge (Firm))
    PR33.D69 1989
    820.7—dc19 88-38100

In Memory of My Mother,
Elizabeth Doyle

Contents

General editor's preface

It is easy to see that we are living in a time of rapid and radical social change. It is much less easy to grasp the fact that such change will inevitably affect the nature of those disciplines that both reflect our society and help to shape it.

Yet this is nowhere more apparent than in the central field of what may, in general terms, be called literary studies. Here, among large numbers of students at all levels of education, the erosion of the assumptions and presuppositions that support the literary disciplines in their conventional form has proved fundamental. Modes and categories inherited from the past no longer seem to fit the reality experienced by a new generation.

New Accents is intended as a positive response to the initiative offered by such a situation. Each volume in the series will seek to encourage rather than resist the process of change; to stretch rather than reinforce the boundaries that currently define literature and its academic study.

Some important areas of interest immediately present themselves. In various parts of the world, new methods of analysis have been developed whose conclusions reveal the limitations of the Anglo-American outlook we inherit. New concepts of literary forms and modes have been proposed; new notions of the nature of literature itself and of how it communicates are current; new views of literature's role in relation to society flourish. *New Accents* will aim to expound and comment upon the most notable of these.

In the broad field of the study of human communication, more and more emphasis has been placed upon the nature and function of the new electronic media. *New Accents* will try to identify and discuss the challenge these offer to our traditional modes of critical response.

The same interest in communication suggests that the series should also concern itself with those wider anthropological and sociological areas of investigation which have begun to involve scrutiny of the nature of art itself and of its relation to our whole way of life. And this will ultimately require attention to be focused on some of those activities which in our society have hitherto been excluded from the prestigious realms of Culture. The disturbing realignment of values involved and the disconcerting nature of the pressures that work to bring it about both constitute areas that *New Accents* will seek to explore.

Finally, as its title suggests, one aspect of *New Accents* will be firmly located in contemporary approaches to language, and a continuing concern of the series will be to examine the extent to which relevant branches of linguistic studies can illuminate specific literary areas. The volumes with this particular interest will nevertheless presume no prior technical knowledge on the part of their readers, and will aim to rehearse the linguistics appropriate to the matter in hand, rather than to embark on general theoretical matters.

Each volume in the series will attempt an objective exposition of significant developments in its field up to the present as well as an account of its author's own views of the matter. Each will culminate in an informative bibliography as a guide to further study. And, while each will be primarily concerned with matters relevant to its own specific interests, we can hope that a kind of conversation will be heard to develop between them; one whose accents may perhaps suggest the distinctive discourse of the future.

TERENCE HAWKES

Introduction:
English and popular culture

Fictional worlds

It seems to us perfectly natural that a group of nationally-organized institutions should select, evaluate, interpret, and stockpile a set of verbal fictions and other imaginative forms of language on our behalf; and furthermore that these institutions should provide for us, and for our children and young people, a mould or framework within which to set our experience of, and relation to these symbolic forms.

In this book I shall attempt to show that the contemporary social status and function of certain fictions, including the specialized kind known as English literature, are in actual fact not natural but contingent, and that this contingency is founded upon a long and contradictory history. Indeed, in education as elsewhere, the movements of the late nineteenth and early twentieth century set many of the mental horizons within which we now operate. It seems that what has become 'second nature' to us is based on the considerable effort of cultural institution-making particularly at the turn of the present century.[1] Since the process of setting up major institutions to channel and stockpile selected fictions was not simply a natural or inevitable phenomenon its apparently self-evident validity can be questioned. Indeed, as will be seen, the actual process of institution-making was historically contradictory and haphazard, and had consequences which were in many respects unpredicted.

In examining this process, I shall attempt to provide answers to the following questions. Why did such institutions come to exist in the first place? What was, and is, their cultural significance? Are alternatives to these institutions desirable or possible?

I have selected the establishment of the modern discipline of English studies in higher education for particular attention since its institutionalization has been national in a more complete sense than any of the other various processes bearing upon the social channelling of fictions. In contrast to fully or partially market-based institutions such as publishing, the theatre, and the modern media, the institution of English studies in British higher education has achieved a significantly more unchallengable or 'normalized' status. While it is possible to conceive of a very different set of institutions within the market-place, it is much more difficult to imagine a system of education in England, Britain, or indeed any English-speaking country which is not founded on the teaching of English. Not only is English currently a central element within the curriculum of higher education (and one for which it has become difficult to conceive of a substitute), it stands as a defining feature of 'basic education' or the 'core curriculum' at school level. But this is a recent development. Prior to the major institutional transformations which took place between 1880 and 1920, the situation was very different.[2]

That this work of institutionalization was considerable becomes clear when we look at the apparently unpropitious raw materials initially available for the purpose. Before 1880 most teaching of languages and literature was either associated with women, or allied to the utilitarian pursuit of functional literacy, and therefore occupied a dramatically lower cultural status than the upper-class masculine studies of Classics and Mathematics. Furthermore, although by the nineteenth century the education of upper-class males was carried out largely through the medium of English, the most valued subject matter (intellectual and symbolic) was contained in, or based upon, works in the classical languages of Latin and Greek. During this period, therefore, the very notion of an academic discipline devoted to the study of English (as opposed to teaching that was incidental to familiarization with the Classics), and especially English literature, would have made little sense within the universities. Looking at the subsequent history one is faced with an unlikely course of events: low status symbolic materials were transformed into a high status discipline which came to occupy a central place within the national curriculum.

In the course of the nineteenth century a fully national system of schooling with predominantly female staff was established throughout Britain. The role given to women within this new national context was itself novel and embodied a conflict of cultural status. There was an unbridgeable gulf between the role of women as homemakers and any professional practice. However, men were unable and unwilling to forge for themselves the kinds of emotional and intellectual skills considered to be necessary to the propagation of 'personal' characteristics among the nation's children. The outcome of this contradictory situation was the establishment of a quasi-maternal semi-profession of the female teacher, rather akin to that of the female nurse. Women teachers were institutionally granted a peculiar capacity for quickening children's personal interests and sense of life-drama, by virtue of what was seen as their instinctive feminine view of the world. With the development of this semi-profession went an investment of value in the teaching of what were called the 'English subjects' (to distinguish them from masculine studies such as Classics). In this way the social use of English literature passed from being a female domestic 'accomplishment' to being a vehicle for the use of female teachers, and thereby also an acceptable element in the teaching of women. The early history of the advanced teaching of English was therefore intimately connected with the entry of women into teaching. It is hardly surprising then that women proved to be not only in a majority within university extension courses in English later in the century, but even that almost all of the students entering the School of English Language and Literature at Oxford (founded in 1893) were female until the First World War (the School was at first given the derisory epithet 'Pink Sunsets' by Oxford men).

In the light of this particular history, subsequent transformations have to be described as remarkable. Thus it is difficult to accept that this history leads seamlessly towards our present system, as most previous accounts have suggested. It was only as a result of much institutional manoeuvring that this intellectually 'second-rate' group of subjects was gradually specialized into its component parts of History, Geography, and English Language and Literature, and each of these was established as a separate department of 'higher' knowledge with professorial status.[3]

In the case of English this institutional elevation was partially the outcome of a 'national demand' which, while grounded on the progress of female education, paradoxically generated increasing provision by the ancient universities for the study of English by men. Most surprisingly of all, this led an unanticipated challenge to the primacy of Classics within the expanding national system of university education. When looked at more closely, it is clear that the institutionalization of English conformed to a pattern familiar in other professional domains, particularly since the nineteenth century. However, the new professional status for English was not achieved without difficulty. Nor did the difficulties and successes of English conform to the development of other modern disciplines. In terms of its eventually achieved overall influence, at both institutional and symbolic levels, the success of English proved to be more dramatic than that of any other subject. Thus by the 1930s it had become fully established as a professional activity within higher education on terms very different from the semi-professional practice of nineteenth-century women teachers. Instead, as will be seen, it became a distinctively male domain, having its own professional modes of research and teaching and ways of controlling admission.

Histories of English

Existing histories bearing on English studies offer little in the way of an explanation of such momentous changes. Instead they tend to impose upon their materials an artificial homogeneity and continuity. For example, literary histories tend to describe the development of English as a sequence of more or less adequate attempts to achieve a direct response to the literary text, and they ignore the particular character of

English as an institutionalized and gendered pedagogic discipline.[4] There are, fortunately, a small number of somewhat more adequate accounts which recognize something of the momentous nature of these early transformations.[5] Their explanations, however, remain couched in terms of an escape from functional origins of English teaching (as moral indoctrination) to a system of study based upon literary texts which have achieved the capacity to promote free growth within the individual ungendered self. This explanation is far from adequate in that it ignores the continuing, if somewhat altered, social functions of the discipline, and provides no account of the social, cultural, and subjective bases of literary value. It is unable to locate any social dynamic underlying the conditions through which a variety of extremely unlikely 'raw materials' were formed into a central academic discipline with its own highly integrated masculine career structure and professional norms. Furthermore, it fails to relate such norms to the development of a distinctive documentary field (consisting of journals, books, and other patterns of publication), or set of professional associations, range of approved pedagogic activities, and mechanisms for the selection of students.

Histories of pre-university English offer a little more insight into the functional changes that have taken place since the nineteenth century, because of their greater underlying concern with current problems of teaching English to school pupils.[6] They also provide some useful information about changes in regulatory mechanisms, such as examinations, syllabuses, and teaching methods. However, even these accounts attempt in various ways to recoup the 'value' and 'growth' model by presenting the history in terms of comparative difficulties and successes in transmitting to working-class pupils a love of literature. Thus, once again, we find recourse to an account of the progressive liberalization of English as it escaped from its nineteenth-century functional moral shackles and moved closer to the more 'civilized' view often assumed to be typified by Cambridge English since the 1920s.[7] Such Whiggish versions tend to present the history as a series of developmental stages. For example, English in schools is seen as having progressed from a rote language grind, to a stage which involved the transmission of a cultural heritage, and finally advanced to the contemporary approach which seeks to encourage in pupils personal growth through experience. Some of the more recent school-based histories have begun to make a significant departure from such developmental approaches, by examining the influence of ideological conflicts within the profession of English teaching upon changes within the discipline.[8] This has allowed the history to be studied in terms of conflicts and compromises at the level of professional consciousness, and has given greater weight to recent challenges to the received assumptions regarding the immanent and inherent value that is said to reside in great literature.

Unfortunately even these histories stop short of examining the relation between the consciousness of professional teachers, and conflicts relating to institutional innovations, state policy, and – most importantly – those wider cultural processes which account for selected fictions having become the object of such large-scale social initiatives in the first place. Interestingly, this limitation can be explained by the genealogy of these same historical accounts. Since they have emerged largely from within English they are shaped in terms of a framework constructed by this discipline itself. Thus they have followed exactly the same cultural divisions, distinctions, and categories of experience that the new discipline propagated and sustained. Furthermore, the acceptance of such received categories has erected firm barriers against the study of the broader social and symbolic relations underlying the dramatic development of the new discipline over the last century or so. Once it had been established as part of a successful modern institution within higher education, English studies excluded from its ambit those wider social processes through which fictions are produced, circulated, and consumed. By legitimizing only the study of 'valuable works', the discipline manufactured an essential and unbridgeable cultural distance between its own sphere of high art and the general domain of popular fiction and discourse.

The altered perspective from which the present account has been written allows us not only to identify the underlying reasons for the gaps within the available writing on the discipline's history, it also calls into question the assumption that English is a perfectly 'normal' and 'natural' field both of cultural production and of study. Indeed, I would suggest that the historical record reveals complex patterns of social and cultural activity within this field whose centre of gravity has shifted radically on a number of occasions. This perspective conflicts fundamentally with the received account of a homogeneous and unified progression towards a 'mature' area of study. Instead, it has become clear to me that beneath the immediate concerns with language, literature, and criticism, much deeper cultural forces have been mobilized in the name of the study of English. If we are to examine these forces we must, as Raymond Williams points out, attend to *all* of the practices that have made up English, including those we have learned to view as marginal.[9] We can begin, as he does, by extending our conception of literature to encompass all 'discourse by writing'. But a further broadening of emphasis is required in order to identify a range of practices of which 'literature' itself, even when defined in this extended manner, is only one kind of example. This takes our analysis well beyond the received discipline-based constraints of English.

A social history of fictions

Perry Anderson's influential essay 'components of the national culture',[10] offers some insight into the processes by which particular forms of discourse, including fictions, have been nationally organized or channelled. Anderson traces the success of English to a factor which he sees as characteristic of wider patterns of cultural hegemony in Britain. In his view, it is the capacity of English studies to articulate systematically a symbolic rather than theoretical totality that has enabled the discipline to occupy a central role in sustaining the 'national culture'. While this accounts at an extremely general level for the discipline's ideological success, the value of Anderson's essay is limited by the narrowness of the conception of 'culture' with which he works. This leads him to treat academic disciplines as if they constituted the 'national culture' as a whole, rather than cultural institutions with a specific kind of national orientation. As applied more carefully by Francis Mulhern,[11] this form of analysis provides a way of understanding how English, as a professionally-chartered discourse on literature, has mediated the entry of a new social layer into the national intelligentsia. But while representing a considerable advance upon those accounts which treat the history of English simply as a history of literature and criticism, Mulhern's book is primarily concerned with the *Scrutiny* movement, and as such tells us little about the discipline's characteristic institutional orientations to nationality, professionalism, and particularly gender. This national dimension has however received some attention elsewhere. According to Macherey and Balibar,[12] a central feature of this kind of nationally-orientated cultural institution is the propagation and maintenance of a sense of an 'imaginary' national educated language made manifest in a set of 'high' fictional discourses. English can thus be seen as an institutionalized set of academic and schooling practices which function to process, evaluate, and transmit works esteemed as having 'cultural value', and – by the same token – to determine which forms of discourse are to count simply as 'ordinary' language and popular fiction. Nevertheless, they fail to note that such educational practices in turn form a part of a broader historical process of the social channelling of fictions.

Such work on national and cultural institutions has important implications since it enables us to understand the history of English studies as an aspect of the wider social production and regulation of fictions. It also allows us to determine the exact nature of the radical gulf between 'vulgar' fictions and a transcendental realm of 'literature' which the discipline of English has played a central part in sustaining. But perhaps we should begin by touching on a central social issue to which the discipline itself oddly enough has paid scant attention: the general role of fictions in society. It seems likely that formal arrangements for the production, circulation, and consumption of verbal fictions (such as stories and other imaginative uses of language) are to be found in all societies. English studies can be seen as but one set of institutions and networks for the channelling of verbal imagining or fiction making. The history of the institutionalization of English can then be understood in terms of larger reorientations of the social functions of fiction making.

In looking at the history from this broader social perspective it is impossible to follow most writers on the subject in separating the social history of English from a history of the power relations involved in symbolic forms. Furthermore, even a brief discussion of the power of symbolic forms requires some general account of the social history of the major types of social network for channelling fictions. Following Attali's account of music,[13] fictions (whether simply narrated, performed or silently read) can be understood as socially-coded types of fantasy. The probably universal social fascination with stories, narratives, and other heightened or ritualized uses of language is related to their capacity to terrify and to harmonize, to act as a symbolic weapon as well as a force for exaltation and transcendence, blasphemy and curse as well as therapy and cure. The overall social importance of fiction making is based upon its ability to engage in symbolic transformations, such as the transformation of anxiety into joy, dissonance into harmony. Indeed through such symbolic transformations, fictions affirm that social order is possible. Thus, a fundamental use value of fictions is their capacity for creating community and reconciliation.

By the same token the social possibilities of fictions render them of interest to those who wield or seek power. Fictional forms have always been put to political uses, and often in ways which alienate the fictions from their basic sources and transform their social value. Attempts to regulate fiction making and consumption seem to arise at an early stage of the implementation of any new order of power, and such attempts may indeed tend towards the achievement of monopoly control. Such appropriations can never be total however, since even politically-harmonized fictional forms are subject to symbolic fragmentation by virtue of their basis in potentially disordered fantasies. My concern here though is more directly with the 'external' or social and cultural influences on the regulation of the making and interpretation of fictions.

It is by now well established that historically different senses of 'culture' relate to different modes of socialization or 'cultivation'. Thus, the lessening during the sixteenth century of the sense of 'worship' associated with the term 'culture' signifies how the process of human cultivation was coming to be associated with processes of social 'breeding' or 'government' (often by means of domestic tuition), rather than ritual.[14] This contained the seeds of a new social relation between fiction making and power, at first through the elevation of selected vernacular forms as suitable for 'breeding' (albeit often only of a 'lighter' kind), and later through the gradual influence of money upon the production, circulation, and use of vernacular 'literature'. The Tudor assimilation of diverse public forms of government to centralized administration and control had encouraged the development of the first truly national sense of country and tongue, at least among the governing classes. This in turn generated a whole sequence of attempts at establishing a 'ruled' or cultured vernacular language tailored to a national system of administration and communication, and the model of the esteemed classical languages of Greece and Rome. 'Literature' came to be understood as limited to those forms of writing which, in their role as 'handmaidens' of the national tongue, were considered to contribute to the classicization process.

Education and modern rhetoric

As relations of money exchange came to predominate, an economic relation based on remuneration for the sale of labour gradually became more generally available to the moulder of fictions. The 'Literary Work' emerged as an object from which an income could be drawn, and patronage now stood as but one among a number of possible economic ties (financial, capitalist, and feudal).[15] At the level of consumption, the autonomous status conferred on literary works by their institutionalization as commodities, was supported by the systematic propagation of new modes of reading. Prescriptions for reading and writing were eventually formally articulated under the rubric of modern rhetoric and *belles-lettres*. An economic as well as cultural network was thereby established which partially simulated ritual community. The literary work was valorized as a symbolic contribution to the maintenance of a harmonious 'high society'. Participation in this literary culture helped sustain the social belief in the reality of a civilization or culture guaranteed by rational exchange rather than worship. As this representational or early capitalist economy progressively broke down the residual networks of ritual and patronage, works of modern English rhetoric and *belles-lettres*, or 'literature', came to be experienced as representing the harmony and order of cultured or 'polite' society, and in this way helped to legitimize by symbolic and fictional means the whole system of power, status, and exchange. In addition, the institutionalization of the literary work as an immaterial commodity enabled merchants to exercise control over literary production, sell its usage, and develop a large pool of customers. In this process the author of literary works (if not of the wider range of 'vulgar' fictions), became an independent entrepreneur offering desirable symbolic commodities to those wishing to develop the kinds of taste required to participate in polite society.

It is this process which underlies the earliest systematic institutionalization of forms of education using vernacular literary works. The teaching of 'Rhetoric and *Belles-Lettres*' was established at first at the margins of power and status in Scotland and the English Dissenting Academies, and eventually found a place in the curriculum of the first English utilitarian college (University College, London, founded in the 1820s) as 'English Language and Literature'.[16] And when university colleges were founded in provincial cities later in the nineteenth century, some provision was usually made for instruction in 'English and History'. Also, from the moment of the establishment in the 1830s of King's College, London as a specifically religious alternative to the utilitarian University College, a much greater emphasis was placed on the role of the 'English subjects' in countering the morally impoverished aspects of Enlightenment rationality. Indeed, the opposition between rationalistic enlightenment and anti-utilitarian moralism came to be inscribed within literary works themselves in the course of the century. From an anti-utilitarian romantic-conservative viewpoint the literary work embodied the values of human relationship and thus transcended exchange value: literature seemed to preserve inspirational, ritual value.

This had particular importance for the social, domestic, and pedagogic links that were forged between women and literature. A strong moral emphasis was to be found in the influential body of writings on female education produced during the eighteenth century. In such writings, vernacular and literary studies were proposed as particularly fitted for women. Despite the development of a 'modern' English form of rhetoric and *belles-lettres*, familiarity with classical knowledge and taste continued to mark out the cultured role of 'gentleman', whereas the cultivation of women could conveniently be restricted to selected

works of vernacular literature, particularly when morally orientated. Since the domestic sphere was also constructed as transcending the male public world of exchange, familiarization
with vernacular literature could be accommodated as a female
domestic 'accomplishment'. It is this history which underlies
the specific association between women, moral education, and
English language and literature which, as has been indicated
above, came to play such an important role later in the
nineteenth century when women were introduced into school
teaching.

On the other hand, if the English subjects were ever to be
elevated to the status of important vehicles for the formal
education of men,[17] they needed to acquire the symbolic and
institutional power to challenge the primacy of classical culture.
Achieving this status was to prove a long and tortuous process,
and one which I shall investigate in detail in chapters 1 and 2.
It should be noted here though, that success also involved what
I shall call the 'nationalization' of English studies. By establishing English as the only academic discipline which embodied
not only the high culture of 'polite society' but also the 'national
character', the discipline came to be promoted as uniquely
suited to a mission of national cultivation. As we shall see, this
conception of English was a major feature of the movement for
institutional innovation launched in the early decades of the
twentieth century. At that stage, 'literature' began to overwhelm 'language' as the defining feature of the higher study of
English. Imaginative and predominantly fictional works were
increasingly culturally esteemed and legitimized as 'literary'
only in so far as they embodied 'manly' as well as 'English'
qualities.[18]

Unlike these 'works' of English literature, popular fictional
forms were only systematically copyrighted and commodified
during the nineteenth century, and produced on a large industrial scale in the twentieth. In this way forms of fiction tailored
to a world of pure exchange, sustained by a star-system of
authorship and a 'popular' consumer market have increasingly
become available. In so far as solvent markets have been
developed for 'popular literature', it has become increasingly
difficult to maintain a set of distinctive principles with which to
insulate 'real' literature from the influence of the 'degradation'

of value through market exchange. At first this distinction was assisted by price differentials and class-based cultural divisions. However, even in the early decades of the twentieth century a dramatic elevation of the importance of literary education was at least partially a response to perceived threats to cultural leadership from 'democratic' and popular economic and cultural processes.

As it happened, the implementation of a mission of national renewal through literary education as proposed in the 1921 Newbolt Report[19] was successfully resisted by the English profession during the inter-war period. But with the increasing dominance of 'popular' markets for symbolic works during the twentieth century, the preservation of a differential framework of value for the demarcation of the truly 'literary' has become increasingly difficult. The disciplinary and discursive adjustments to this difficulty as the century has progressed provide the context for the successive crises articulated through quite hysterical debates on the nature of literary value.

English and political economy

Measuring the value of things has always been the central problem of political economy.[20] In the market, differential pricing can publicly signify relative values to some extent, but the problem of ensuring popular acceptance of exchange as a rational basis for all value remains. Thus, education and culture (and indeed religion) have been constructed as repositories of value prior to exchange. But this presents major problems for the making of national educational and cultural institutions: how can a nationally-orientated system be prevented from undermining all exchange value? Given the intractability of this problem, any national (as opposed to class-based) system of education must have some means of injecting value into the national culture so as to counter the aridity of purely quantitative rationality and exchange. Political economy, and indeed Science, are themselves too bound up with quantitative rationality to perform this task, which therefore falls to their apparent polar opposite 'Culture'. With the efforts to initiate national forms of education later in the nineteenth century, discourses on 'culture' provided an important site for transitions between 'classical' and 'modern' forms of general education. At first, the national orientation as it affected English in universities was directed towards a revitalization of leadership qualities. Thus discourses and educational practices based on 'Culture' helped ensure that English studies could combine personal value with cultural attributes of a caste of leaders.

The investment of the formal study of the 'English classics' with 'cultural' qualities was the dramatic change attempted here. Only in this way could English studies became the most important academic disciplinary repository of 'Culture', and be able to offer some kind of resolution to the problems posed in quantifying value through exchange. Subsequently English has been established as the central modern academic discipline legitimized to provide and sustain a basis for symbolic exchange value. Through institutionalization as an academic discipline, selected literary works were seemingly removed from the context of abstract generalized exchange, and fitted to affirm the existence of intrinsic value prior and external to exchange. This explains the centrality of questions of 'literary value' within English.[21] This issue is important for the discipline not so much because it helps sustain an inherent value for literature itself, but because in so doing it provides an apparently self-sustaining transcendental (objective) ground for *all* use and exchange values.

The simulation of ritual community

As a result of significant transformations in the relationship between conceptions of English culture (and particularly in its orientations to nationality, class, and gender) and the study of English, new networks were built and to some extent instituted. In this process the study of English was invested with a value which sprang from its capacity to simulate ritual community (or 'society' in the narrow sense) rather than rationalized exchange. In Britain this took the form not so much of a 'nationalization' of the writing process (although English studies would affect this also), but of the sifting and comparative evaluation of literary works, ways of reading, and the production of critical commentary; in sum, institutionalizing a system by which rankings and comparative assessments of fictional forms (forms of symbolic signification) might be established.

This is what was involved in the nationalization of culture through English literary education. It explains the urgency with which disciplinary energies were invested in a series of struggles to define (palpably and qualitatively rather than quantitatively) the stuff of English culture or sensibility. This remained true of the Leavisian project of using literature, as the embodied wisdom of the past, to recreate in pupils the (revalued and narrowed) English 'tradition', and thereby check the present excesses of a utilitarian society.

Graham Hough has been almost unique among writers within the discipline in realizing that this project implied an aspiration to gauge the whole condition of intellectual health in the national life.[22] Within the tendency represented by Richards, Leavis, and the *Scrutiny* movement, exposure to works of literature was presented as an antidote to the reduction of all meaning and value to quantitative money exchange. English studies became the repository of a 'national conscience' which aspired to shape and control the mutations of the national popular imagination and thus resist the 'blind' and otherwise 'uncontrollable forces' which the system had itself unleashed and exploited. In this respect, English has been a greater force for the legitimization of social 'value' than its manifest concern with literature and criticism suggests. This lies behind the subsequent disciplinary imperative to establish evaluative purpose and criteria. As an ever greater requirement is placed upon the discipline to resolve problems of quantifying exchange value, the discipline has itself entered a condition of accelerating crisis. While even today much critical discourse is driven by an imperative towards symbolic harmonization this has taken the form of increasingly desperate attempts to reduce disparate and dissonant fictions to some kind of simulacrum of harmonic unity.

I should like to thank Peter Widdowson, Peter Brooker, Michael Green, and Terence Hawkes without whose support I could certainly not have energized myself over such a long period to complete this project; and to Terry Lovell whose words of encouragement at a crucial moment, helped motivate me in the latter stages. There is a way in which the present book results from the emergence of a larger movement of critics, teachers, and students which over the past decade or so has been actively concerned with reconsidering and challenging the received wisdom about the actual and desirable relationships between literature, teaching, and politics. Many of the central concerns of this movement are recorded in two previous volumes in this series, *Re-Reading English* and *Re-Writing English*. While no direct authorial responsibility for the present work should be attributed to this collective effort, it would gratify me to think that I have in some way contributed to providing a general and historical framework within which our debates might continue and advance, particularly at this moment of often dispiriting reaction.

English literature
and cultural identities

The crisis of leadership

The mechanisms through which a cultural and institutional identity for English studies was established were forged within a wider social movement which developed between the 1880s and the 1920s. This movement, for which the English Association provides our focal point, was in turn directly dependent upon wider contemporary cultural and institutional initiatives and experiments having as their target greater social efficiency. During this period of arrested imperial expansion and international competition many influential figures and associations took the view that the achievement of such social efficiency required a renewal of cultural leadership at a national level.[1] This new cultural leadership was articulated in terms of a spiritual character or aura which would elicit consent on the part of the governed, and was of immense influence for the early development of the institutionalized discipline of English studies. Indeed, the whole period is marked by a series of attempts to define what specific kinds of leadership qualities would be needed to maintain the overseas empire as well as ensuring secure government at home. It involved spasmodic attempts at boosting advanced teaching and research in science and other fields of 'modern' study, especially as applied to industrial organization and technological development. More consistently though, the machinery of an expanded state engaged with general initiatives in the sphere of 'culture', including non-scientific forms of education.

On the whole these efforts carried a national emphasis, as a number of educationalists, politicians, philosophers, and political theorists searched for new and more efficient ways of building and disseminating a national sense of ancestry, tradition, and universal 'free' citizenship. However, the cultural negotiations involved were problematic since they generated tensions between individualism and the investment of cultural authority in the state. Furthermore, while a revitalized ruling and administering class might be seen to require infusions of men of wealth and leadership from slightly lower social layers, this could prove acceptable only under conditions in which new procedures for educational cultivation had been established. Although it had become easier for some middle-class men (or their sons) to earn membership of the national ruling culture by Edwardian times, their status as true 'gentlemen' remained equivocal in an atmosphere of continued mistrust of the business community, albeit tempered by outbreaks of anxiety over the volatility of the lower orders which it was felt the task of their middle-class superiors to defuse.[2]

Thus, the period between 1880 and 1920 was marked by a sequence of strategies to combine under the loose banner of 'efficiency' traditions of aristocratic cultural mystique with utilitarian programmes of industrial and social administration. From this perspective, the working class was seen as the object for colonization by its cultural superiors in order that 'respectable' members of the class be separated from their 'rough' residue, and the leaders of the class be made fit for a limited role in governing the nation.[3] In this process any shadows of socialist organization were to be dispersed by the radiance of a common culture and heritage. The nation was organized not only in class terms but also in terms of gender and age. It was conceived as the proper function of the nation's mothers to rear (within families suitably inoculated against any possibility of communism in the home)[4] fine imperial specimens of manhood. Schooling also had a central place in such initiatives. As a crucial feature of their role in cultural reproduction, schools were expected to inculcate in the nation's children a proper sense of patriotic moral responsibility. In so far as schooling proved too 'mechanical' a procedure for influencing the pupils' subjectivities in the approved manner,[5] efforts were also made to influence home life in a more direct fashion. This was a tendency which coincided with the elimination of mothers and young children from employment in the wake of technological innovations which particularly diminished the kinds of work in which traditionally they had participated.[6]

In many ways the Settlement movement of the 1880s and 1890s provided test sites for these initiatives. Here young men (some of whom, such as C. E. Vaughan,[7] subsequently supported the elevation of English within the national system of education), fired by a somewhat secularized 'politics of conscience', engaged in missionary work addressed to the cultural colonization of the great mass of the excluded population.[8] Deep in the heartland of 'unknown England' that was London's East End, they tested their aura of cultural mystique against the potentially demystifying pressures of the East End world.[9] It was upon this forcing-ground that those traditional modes of cultural authority, reinforced by an Oxbridge education, could systematically be reworked in such a way as to govern (or professionally administer) a class-divided industrial society.[10]

The new modes of official and semi-official supervision and government are best viewed in terms of a general 'collectivist' modification of older patterns of 'individualism'. In attempting to develop a new collective sense of Englishness, intellectuals and administrators alike applied themselves to what, at an earlier (and indeed later) time would have been seen as an 'un-English' and idealist version of the national life. This vision was directly concerned with the governing of an (at least potentially) spiritually organic and mechanically efficient nation. In its more philosophical aspects such intellectual work was addressed to providing a theoretical underpinning for a collectivist social outlook which would be immune equally from the mechanical vulgarities of statism and the revolutionary demands of socialism.[11] It was only in the context of the theoretical work of T. H. Green and Bernard Bosanquet, and of Fabian 'municipal' revisions of the programme of socialism, that William Harcourt, the prominent Liberal politician, could claim in the 1890s that 'we're all socialists now'. The new philosophy of society moved beyond any simple vision of the state as a set of administrative institutions, towards a vision of it as an almost venerable ideal form: a form which claimed to be able to dissolve political struggle in the larger flow of the national way of life, in the name of common culture and common economic interest.[12]

At a more practical level, but under the shadow of such an ideal, went the building of a series of administrative layers at the sensitive ideological point between the official state and the mass of the people. It is, indeed, at this very point that the movement to advance the status of 'English' in education must be situated if its particular history as a cultural and administrative form is to be understood. The advancement of the newly invented discipline of English must thus be examined in the context of a growth in the number of semi-autonomous professions in fields like public administration and welfare, journalism, publicity, and the arts, and of the establishment of national cultural institutions geared to providing a schedule for organizing the nation.

From classics to English

It was only during the early decades of the present century that English studies (or, more simply, 'English') in its recognizably modern disciplinary form began to offer an educationally significant challenge to the intellectual and cultural prestige long invested in classics. As MacPherson has argued, the elevation of the vernacular language and literature within higher education was an attempt to sustain the notion of a 'liberal education' in the face of tendencies towards academic specialization on the one hand, and the dwindling popularity of classics on the other. The introduction of the national language and literature at Oxbridge was seen (at least to begin with) as a broadening and rejuvenation of the 'literary' curriculum which would thereby be sustained as a foundation for more specialized study.[13] Benjamin Jowett (1817–93), Master of Balliol College, Oxford, and one of the modernizing dons who supported endeavours to extend university education and to attract men from new social classes to Oxford, considered that 'classical study is getting in some respects worn out, and the plan proposed [the introduction of English Language and Literature at Oxford] would breathe new life into it'.[14]

One of the signs of the eclipse of classics by English was the foundation in 1907 of the English Association which was to propound very effectively the view that the new discipline had become 'our finest vehicle for a genuine humanistic education' and that 'its importance in this respect was growing with the disappearance of Latin and Greek from the curricula of our schools and universities'.[15] However, the eventual transference from the classical curriculum to a modern alternative, and the enhancement of English and Englishness which was one of its major products, drew on the raw materials provided by the scholarly work of the middle decades of the nineteenth century. In the process of inventing the new English, these materials were substantially transformed to serve a national and imperial culture. In fact, it was only as a consequence of this earlier work of literary, linguistic, and historical categorizing that it became possible for a sense of national and vernacular 'ancestry' to challenge the cultural and educational rule of the classical languages and literatures. Arthur Quiller-Couch, in a lecture given while he was Professor of English Literature at Cambridge in 1916, recalled the impact of this challenge on his contemporaries several decades earlier:

> Few in this room are old enough to remember the shock of awed surprise which fell upon young minds presented, in the late 'seventies and early 'eighties of the last century with Freeman's *Norman Conquest* or Green's *Short History of the English People*; in which as through parting clouds of darkness, we beheld our ancestry, literary as well as political, radiantly legitimised.[16]

New cultural strategies

We can now attend to some of the specific ways in which these general initiatives were worked through, from an explicitly cultural standpoint. The notion of 'degeneracy' is important in this context. Around and within this notion a constant play with gender, nationality, self, age, and maturity can be traced. The esteemed characteristics were those associated with masculinity, activity and concrete statement, and personal poise and self-mastery, together with a concern for racial purity or at least racial vigour. Variants of social Darwinism were used to authorize British competition with other nations, attempts at racial perfectibility, and preferred notions of essential human subjectivity. For example, the idea of advanced education as a process for the 'regeneration of the self' was strongly propounded by modernizing Oxbridge dons like Mark Pattison, an influential educationalist and Head of Lincoln College, Oxford from 1861.[17] For Pattison the essence of the human self (essential subjectivity) was the passive human subject produced by 'nature'. However, a truly 'liberal' or 'higher' education could inculcate a higher subjectivity which transcended nature by offering experiences, feelings, and pleasures that were beyond the mindless routines thought to be engaged in by most of mankind.[18] The 'culture' offered by a liberal education could thus control nature by generating a higher form of 'life' – by teaching 'the art to live'.[19]

This whole cultural ensemble was held together in a manner which bore a striking resemblance to ways of dealing with statism and socialism which have been considered above. Collectivist strategies attempted to restrain any tendencies towards statism or socialism by tempering the full rigours of *laissez-faire* capitalism through a renewal of state and semi-state institutions. In the case of general cultural strategies, the excesses of full-blown conceptions of social Darwinism were qualified by re-interpreting self-governing natural processes as capable of cultural modification (as in Pattison's scheme). This led to a considerable investment of energy in shaping from above the constituents of the national culture and national character; and to the identification and removal of any tendencies towards degeneration within the national 'body'.

These procedures played a central part in the construction of the new English. They could not, however, have been sustained without the development of parallel general educational initiatives of unprecedented scope. It is important here, though, not to take the notion of 'education' in any narrow sense, since the mission of national education as it operated between 1880 and 1920 encompassed institutions, events, and locations well beyond the scope of education as it has since come to be formally conceived. Education took place not only in schools and colleges, but in the home and at local and national gatherings (as in the case of the National Home Reading Union);[20] at public galleries and museums; and even within city streets, in the signifying processes encouraged through the erection of monuments of a national flavour in prominent positions within the urban landscape.[21] Nor was the rural landscape omitted from such initiatives: the National Trust was founded in 1895 to secure the permanent preservation of places and buildings of 'beauty' and of 'historic' interest; that is, to sustain the national heritage in its physical and geographical aspects. In 1897 a permanent site for British works of art was established as the National Gallery of Modern Art (Tate Gallery) at Millbank, London, to display as well as preserve approved works of visual art. Similarly the National Portrait Gallery, which was permanently established in 1896, and the *Dictionary of National Biography* (1885–1900) stand as counterparts at the level of individual portrayal and biography, to the work of categorization and charting that went into producing monumental works on the national history, language, and literature such as the *Cambridge History of English Literature* (1907–16) and the *New* (later *Oxford*) *English Dictionary* (1884–1928).

Even within more formal patterns of education, initiatives ranged from those which tended increasingly towards the institutionalization of a national system overseen by the state (Education Acts from 1870 to 1902 and beyond; the formation of School Boards and Education Authorities and a national Board of Education (1899)) to a number of semi-state programmes such as, from the 1870s, the national 'extension movement', the National Council of Adult Schools Association, and later, the Workers' Educational Association. The English Association should also be mentioned here since it showed a considerable overlap of personnel and policies with many of these other initiatives (formal and informal), having particularly close affinities with the National Home Reading Union, the *Dictionary of National Biography*, and the National Trust, and occupying an interesting position of relative autonomy from the state Board of Education.

The new English

Specific developments within formal education and their relation to the new English can now be given direct attention. The period saw transformations (mooted from the 1850s) of modes of professional academic organization and administration, teaching, research, and publication. In general such transformations involved secularization as much as professionalization and operated not only inwards towards the academy but also outwards towards a new constituency: the nation as a whole. A partial eclipse of religious belief in the face of social relations organized around industry, science, and technology, led to greater emphases on a 'lay' ministry and pedagogy, and a search, from the mid nineteenth century, for new tools of a general higher education.[22] Oxbridge institutions, though, were slow to respond to such trends and it was only towards the end of the century that calls from the ancient universities to accept a 'national' role began to be heeded. By the turn of the century Oxbridge was beginning to service a limited amount of social mobility; but, on the whole, middle-class education continued to be catered for elsewhere, increasingly through the 'extension movement' (see pp. 28–30) and the 'provincial' colleges.[23] The challenge by versions of 'science' to the classical curriculum has been mentioned above but one way of dealing with this challenge should be identified here. This was articulated by the scientist, educationalist, and parliamentarian Lyon Playfair at a meeting to publicize the establishment of York College in 1875:

> Our universities cannot get hold of our great industrial centres in any permanent way unless they raise them in self-respect and dignity by giving them an intellectual understanding of their vocations . . . [They] have not learned that the stronghold of literature should be in the upper classes of society, while the stronghold of science should be in the nation's middle class.[24]

The 'literature' to which Playfair refers is, of course, classics rather than English literature (which had not yet come to be seen as an adequate instrument of 'culture'). In fact, it was largely through the middle-class and scientific bias of the new provincial colleges that English Language, Literature, and History came to serve as a so-called 'poor man's classics', and it was only at the very end of the century that Oxbridge became sufficiently concerned to begin to succumb to the then 'national demand'[25] for such studies and introduce new 'Schools' and 'Tripos' regulations that would allow the ancient institutions to take a lead in these new areas. Oxbridge, then, was only lifted to the apex of the study of English language, literature, and history when it was subjected to the demands for national efficiency and leadership.

The foundation of a national Board of Education signalled the acceptance within the official culture of a need for policies that would co-ordinate an efficient and fully national system of education, and also allowed the voices of dons who had been calling for a transformation of the traditional curriculum to carry more weight than ever before. The 'English subjects' proved particularly attractive here. The 1904 School Regulations refer to 'the group of subjects commonly classed as "English" and including the English language and literature, Geography and History'.[26] In contrast, a circular of the Board published in 1920, 'The teaching of English in Secondary Schools', deals with 'English' solely under the headings of 'Literature' and 'Composition'. Literature is introduced as follows: 'Real knowledge and appreciation of Literature come only from first-hand study of the works of great writers. The first thing to be done is to draw up a list of such works to be read in school.' And composition is also indebted to literature:

> Composition means arrangements, and English composition is the arrangement, in speaking or writing English, of right words in their right order, so as to convey clearly a consecutive meaning. It thus involves the arrangement, not merely of words, but of the substance of thought which the words are meant to convey. . . . Only through composition can pupils acquire effective mastery of the enlarged vocabulary with which they become acquainted through literature, but which remains inert in their minds without the exercise of applying it to the expression of their own thought.[27]

With the increase of tension between universal education and differential provision, the special qualities of the new English (under the hegemony of English literature) for securing the sense of a common culture while at the same time being suited to differential application across the range of educational sectors, caused the Board to look very kindly on the fledgling discipline and to give a great deal of support to its advancement in schools.[28]

'English', then, by the first decade of the new century, had come to have a multi-faceted character due to its variation of role within the new provincial colleges, Oxbridge, and the national system of schooling. From the 1850s miscellaneous 'general knowledge' about the language, literature, and history had been considered as appropriate content for examining potential recruits to the Civil Service, and especially the Indian Civil Service. By 1875 seventeen examinations were available to schoolboys covering not only the Civil Service, but also the Armed Forces, the professions, and the universities, in nearly all of which the English subjects were set.[29] Thus, at least at this level, the English subjects were already well established as minimal testing devices for entry into state, semi-state, and autonomous professional organizations. The study of language, literature, and history was also substantially influenced by the general process of higher academic specialization which took place during the same period. University College London, and Owen's College, Manchester were the earliest influences in this respect. Here, apart from reliance on the rigours of a large-scale examination system, new areas of modern knowledge were set up as autonomous academic disciplines with a related German-style system of professoriate, administrative hierarchy, and departmental structure, and a commitment to research – none of which was characteristic of the operations of the traditional classical curriculum.[30]

English Language, Literature, and History in the colleges was both similar to and different from these other modern disciplines; similar in that, like them, it sought to create for itself a solid and autonomous identity; different (especially from the early decades of this century) in that its predominantly classi-cally-trained and often clerical academic proponents in-creasingly claimed for it a status well beyond that of any mere 'discipline' or 'knowledge subject'. The history of the transition from 'English Language and Literature', 'English and History', and 'English subjects' to the simple and all-embracing generic term 'English' is the history of a complex process of cultural extension and elevation. 'English' came to extend its range of operations beyond any disciplinary boundaries to encompass all mental, imaginative, and spiritual faculties. In the words of one professor, the object of teaching English literature came to be not the imparting of 'knowledge' but 'the cultivation of the mind, the training of the imagination, and the quickening of the whole spiritual nature.[31] English was elevated through being imbued with the kind of cultural authority previously invested in classics, but now with the addition of a powerful national dimension that yet somehow transcended nationality. According to another professor:

> literature should be a means of larger experience – a conning tower or an upper chamber with a view beyond bounds of class, locality, time or country. . . . It was clear that literature deepened our sense of the import of nationality by giving the most intense and at the same time most manifold expression of it.[32]

By the early decades of this century English was being called upon to sustain a 'national ideal' – an ideal which was traced back to Matthew Arnold. Its role was to assist in the educational work of transcending 'individual self-interest' by subordinating the 'individual self' to 'common aims':

> In his educational outlook [Arnold] was a nationalist. . . . Such an ideal, he believed, could be imparted and maintained by a public system of education. . . . Matthew Arnold's great achievement was that he convinced the younger generation among his readers of the necessity for providing throughout England an abundant supply of public secondary schools for boys and girls, schools which would be intellectually competent, attested by public inspection, and aided both by local authorities and the state.[33]

In serving this ideal, one feature which gave the new English its peculiar potency was the cultural mystique endowed upon it by a vision of the qualities seen as inherent in the national literature. This vision was most dramatically evoked by John Bailey at a conference of the English Association in 1917:

> [Bailey] related a story of an officer who read the *Fairie Queen* to his men when they were in a particularly difficult situation. The men did not understand the words, but the poetry had a soothing influence upon them. Nothing better could be said of poetry than that.[34]

In order to understand the genesis of this new cultural form, we must examine some other forces of cultural extension and elevation which provided its preconditions. The history of the 'extension movement' illustrates many of the cultural patterns which influenced the emergence of the new English.

The moves for an extended system of university education reach back to the 1840s when it was aimed at providing more qualified candidates for Anglican ordination, but it was very soon transformed into a more lay-oriented mission. The first practical measures of educational extension were instituted during the 1850s and 1860s when London degrees were opened to all who could pass an 'external' examination, but it was only towards the end of the 1860s that an emphasis on English language, literature, and history became an important feature of the process of extension. In the course of the next two decades Oxford and Cambridge became involved in what one of the Cambridge extension lecturers described as an attempt to provide 'University Education for the Whole Nation by an itinerant system connected with the Old Univesities'.[35] The object of this peripatetic programme from the point of view of Oxbridge was outlined by the Oxford Vice-Chancellor in 1887:

> The lecturers whom we send through the country are a kind of missionary; wherever they go they carry on their foreheads the name of the University they represent. To a great majority of those persons with whom they come in contact it is the only opportunity afforded of learning what Oxford means and what is meant by the powers of an Oxford education.[36]

Of course, what Oxford 'meant' and the source of its 'powers', a classical curriculum taught within an intimate collegiate system, could hardly be extended. The new 'meaning', therefore, that was preached by the missionaries was embodied in a modern subject: English Language, Literature, and History. The ideal of a complete integration of the cultural mission of the universities with English was to be most clearly articulated in the pages of the Newbolt Report of 1921, *The Teaching of English in England*, which is examined in detail in chapter 2 (pp. 41–67).[37] But in these earlier days, English was not without rivals.

T. H. Green, first chairman of Oxford extension lectures in 1879, favoured a philosophical system which would 'appeal both to the intelligence and to the emotion', and thereby provide 'a rational view of man and society, a theory neither hedonist nor materialist'.[38] Even if Philosophy never gained the role Green hoped that it would, Benjamin Jowett was remarkably successful in inculcating his latter-day Platonic guardians at Green's Oxford college, Balliol, with a renewed vision of leadership. Green's own views carried a good deal of influence within another 'extension movement', the 'settlements', set up from the 1880s in London's East End and other urban areas. The view of citizenship which Green promulgated, and which was supported by Jowett's successor as Master of Balliol, Caird, was influential in forming the social ideals of a generation of politicians, senior Civil Servants (including those within the Board of Education), and influential members of the English Association.

The settlement movement has been mentioned above. The orientation here was more 'collectivist' and it can be seen as a response to socialist challenges to policies based on political economy and philanthropy. The settlement of Toynbee Hall in the East End of London was founded in 1884 by the Christian socialist Samuel Barnett. The settlement connects with other forms of extension in that it did have an educational aim, but, like Oxford House (another settlement or 'mission' set up in the East End in 1884), it usefully illustrates new initiatives for the renewal of forms of leadership and patterns for social administration upon which the elevation of English largely depended. Barnett saw Toynbee Hall as the potential centre for an east London university; in fact it became, as did the other settlements and extension classes, a centre for members of the middle class.[39] While Toynbee Hall 'expressed the spirit of Balliol', Oxford House came out of the more 'missionary' Keble College, Oxford.[40] Indeed the Federation of Working Men's Clubs set up by Oxford House directly assisted the young Oxford missionary in developing the 'knack of mingling on terms of personal equality with men, while yet by some *je ne sais quoi* in himself', preserving 'their freely accorded social homage'.[41] This was as much the true 'meaning' of Oxford as was any other aspect of the programme of extension. What was at stake was the renovation of modes for achieving freely-given cultural consent to a renewed leadership; a leadership capable of entering the world of 'men' on terms of only apparent equality. The first annual report of the Oxford House mission in 1884 set this programme out most clearly: 'Colonisation by the well-to-do seems indeed the true solution to the East End question, for the problem is, how to make the masses realise their spiritual and social solidarity with the rest of the capital and the kingdom.' The report goes on to claim that the people could only be taught 'thrift and prudence' by men who would actually associate with them, thereby ensuring that the influence of 'the imperishable youth of Oxford' would 'induce them to face the elementary laws of economics'.[42]

The same ideological pattern is to be found within the imperial, educational, and commercial programme for 'national efficiency' which, from the 1890s, drew in a number of prominent figures from the worlds of politics, business, and 'letters'.[43] John Gorst, Conservative MP, intimate of Samuel Barnett, and a supporter of this programme, captured the emotions that motivated this ideology when speaking at Glasgow University in 1894. In his view the crowding of 'the destitute classes' into the cities had made 'their existence thereby more conspicuous and dangerous', particularly since they 'already form a substantial part of the population, and possess even now, although they are still ignorant of their full power, great political importance'. The danger was that they might even go beyond 'their lawful power at the polls', especially if stirred up by 'designing persons' and promises of 'social salvation', and they might attempt to produce change through 'revolutionary action'.[44] Barnett himself saw the solution to the problem in achieving an amicable peace between rich and poor by finding the cultural means of bringing together the 'two nations'.[45] R. B. Haldane, another important member of the 'national efficiency group', was also a keen supporter of extension programmes, and future Lord Chancellor in both Liberal and Labour governments. His views show how the proponents of national efficiency linked together a concern for a renewal of leadership qualities with the generation of a cultural mystique through education. In the course of his rectorial address at Edinburgh in 1907, Haldane asserted that 'when a leader of genius comes forward the people may bow down before him, and surrender their wills, and eagerly obey', since 'to obey the commanding voice was to rise to a further and wider outlook, and to gain a fresh purpose'. To this end, students must live for their work: 'So only can they make themselves acepted leaders; so only can they aspire to form a part of that priesthood of humanity to whose commands the world will yield obedience.'[46]

The English Association (also founded in 1907) applied itself to the advancement of the new English within the national culture. One of the principal figures within the Association was to be Henry Newbolt, imperialist poet, celebrant of the mystique of the public school, future chairman of the Board of Education Committee which reported on the state of English in 1921, and – like Haldane – a supporter of the national efficiency group in its aims of planning imperial policy, improving education, and recapturing commercial prosperity.[47]

Culture, society, and the English Association

The English Association was set up to promote the maintenance of 'correct use of English, spoken and written', the recognition of English as 'an essential element in the national education', and the discussion of teaching methods and advanced study as well as the correlation of school with university work.[48] From the beginning, personnel attached to the new Board of Education seem to have been sympathetic to the view of English as the most natural candidate to lead a mission of cultural renewal: at any rate, from its inception the English Association set out to ensure that such was the case. George Saintsbury, Professor of Rhetoric and English Literature at Edinburgh, in his presidential address to the AGM of the Scottish branch in 1907, emphasized the importance of bringing the influence of the Association to bear on questions of education when they came before the legislature. In this way the Association 'might really be the means of exercising a not inconsiderable leverage on

educational performance and educational arrangements'.[49]
Within a few years firm and formal contacts with the Board of
Education had been established. Arthur Acland, the Liberal
politician and president of the Association, announced in 1910
that the Board of Education 'would welcome help from us in
putting forward a scheme for English teaching in Secondary
Schools'.[50] This was confirmed by a statement carried in the
next bulletin of the Association:

> The Board of Education has now given effect to the intima-
> tion conveyed by Mr. Acland and vaguely announced by him
> at the Annual meeting. They have definitely asked for re-
> presentatives of the Association to confer with their officers in
> order to discuss a circular which they are preparing on the
> teaching of English in secondary schools. In this way, for the
> first time, the Association obtains official recognition.[51]

In 1917 the Association was largely responsible for convinc-
ing the Board of the need for a Departmental Committee to
investigate the state of the teaching of English in England, and
to propose plans for future developments. When the Committee
was subsequently formed, eight of its fourteen members were
from the Association.[52] The new Association is best seen not so
much as a pressure group founded to further the professional
interests of teachers of English, but rather as a class-based
mobilization which drew in not only most professors of English
Language and Literature, but also like-minded politicians,
administrators, and 'men of letters'. In the person of the
(non-academic) Henry Newbolt, who subsequently was to
chair the Departmental Committee, it found a figure who could
articulate many of the themes to which both the fledgling
discipline and the Association itself adhered. Newbolt was
quick to express his hostility to the whole notion of formal
'institutions'. When about to become a member of the Association in 1913, a commentator wrote of him:

> Nothing in the world caused him such dismay, such instant
> feelings of antagonism, as catching sight of any institution
> whatsoever. . . . He was coming inside the English Associ-
> ation with the hope of assuring himself that his own principles
> were being carried out by it.[53]

As a writer on the early days of the Association subsequently noted, the movement tended to work by modes of informal 'social lubrication'.[54] Throughout the years up to the publication of the 1921 Report, the Association had a policy of alternating the occupants of its presidential chair between men of letters (such as Saintsbury, Bradley, Ker, Herford, and Gosse) and representatives of the official parliamentary culture (including Acland, Balfour, Morley, and Asquith). It also at various times gathered into its ambit important figures within general educational administration (for example, Haddow, Sadler, Barker, Curzon, Mansbridge, and a host of college Heads, Registrars Provosts, and Vice-Chancellors). Perhaps the Association derived its authority from its ability to mobilize such a wide diversity of influential persons on the basis of its anti-institutional stance.

In bringing into relation such pesonnel, the Association also brought together the cultural and institutional themes that have been detailed above. Members of the Association recognized, for example, potential dangers arising from the loss of aristocratic leadership, and the rise of a cultural market-place which urgently necessitated the use of literary culture to bring about an apparently spontaneous consent to a regenerated leadership. As one speaker at the AGM of 1909 said:

> The old standards have decayed, the aristocracy no longer take the intellectual lead; men of letters and booksellers are left face to face with a multitude of readers whose intellectual appetites and tastes are emancipated from all direct influence and control. If we look at the state of our imaginative literature, we must observe in it a grossness, even an indecency, of conception, and an inflowing tide of slang and vulgarity and other forms of ugliness which tend to corrupt imagination and barbarize language. These are the inevitable results of leaving the merit of a book to be determined exclusively by market value.[55]

But it was also recognized that such circumstances called for different strategies within the respective elementary and higher sectors of education. While for elementary pupils the object was to instil a feeling for the grandeur of the national language and literature, within the higher sector it was felt to be necessary to fire the pupils' and students' imaginations: to provide indirect moral inculcation through pleasurable and even joyous responses to literary values.[56] The Association applied itself to ways of resolving the continuing tension between the utilitarian needs of business and industry and the reinvigoration of a cultural leadership, its avowed objective being to reconcile practical utility, enlightened patriotism, and the 'human ideal' in education.[57] F. W. Moorman, Professor of English Language at Leeds and an active supporter of the Workers' Educational Association, told the annual conference in 1914 that the main purpose of the teaching of English literature was not to impart knowledge, or to 'equip students for the conquest of the world'; indeed, the object was not to 'teach' at all but to 'delight' and, 'for some, to sweeten leisure'.[58] Compare this with the substance of the motion moved by P. J. Hartog, Academic Registrar of University College London, on behalf of the Association at the Federal Conference of Education in 1907:

> the object of the teaching of English should be to develope [sic] in pupils the power of thought and expression, and the power of appreciating the content of great literary works, rather than to inculcate a knowledge of grammatical, philological and literary detail.[59]

Such an objective involved establishing what, in practice, were to stand as the proper constituents of the new English, and their relation to each other. The record of debates within the Association reveals the gradual emergence of 'literature' (sometimes used as a synonym for 'poetry') at first as an essential feature of English, and then as its primary constituent. The debate which followed Hartog's motion took the form of a 'heated controversy' over the relative merits of grammar, philology, and literary detail as opposed to the contents of great works.

Another debate during this early period revolved around the actual terms (and their implications) being used to describe the new discipline. C. H. Herford, Professor of English Literature at Manchester, pointed out in 1918 that 'English' or 'English Language and Literature' was 'a loose name for a group of studies differing in educational aim, and in the faculties they appealed to, and those they demanded for successful prosecution'. None the less, these studies had two chief aspects: the science of language and literature, and the medium of a 'broader culture'.[60] In general, though, there was a clear movement towards replacing 'English Language and Literature' and the 'English Subjects' with the simple all-embracing term 'English', and this went with the assumption of a new focus. English was essentially seen as concerned with the contents of 'great works' and as the medium for transmitting a 'broader culture', which meant establishing a dominant role for literature. The conception of the centrality of literature could be tacitly and uncontroversially assumed in a 1919 bulletin of the Association where the general goal of promoting 'the exact study of our literature which the English Association has at its heart' is simply stated as self-evident.[61]

However, while for members of the Association literature was an end in itself and a source of pleasure, it was also a vehicle for morality.[62] In fact, the ultimate source of value in literature as in society was moral authority. The force of this moral authority becomes clearer when discussions within the Association touching specifically upon the pedagogic uses of literature and indeed language are considered. Here the double emphasis upon the need to arrest cultural degeneration and preserve the national heritage was distinctly in evidence.

For example, the critic and essayist John Bailey was a figure who linked the National Trust with the English Association in his concern equally for the heritage and literary values. Bailey was chairman of the Association from 1912 to 1915, and president in 1925–6. He was also a key figure in the National Trust and chairman of its executive committee between 1912 and 1931. At a meeting of the Association in 1913, Bailey was described by Caroline Spurgeon (the first woman to be appointed to a British university professorship in arts – she was a University of London Professor of English Literature at Bedford College from 1913 – and a member of the Newbolt Committee) as 'a treasure keeper' in his role as 'a custodian of some of the greatest and most precious national possessions, England's places of historical interest and beauty'. Had it not been for him and his colleagues at the National Trust many old and historical buildings would have suffered. Now, as chairman of the English Association, 'he was but widening the sphere of his watchfulness'.[63] The care which Bailey lavished on his 'treasures' within the National Trust was at least equalled by his work as activist and propagandist for the 'eternal values' of poetry through the Association and in the pages of the Newbolt Report where his contribution to the section on the universities was particularly notable.[64]

For Bailey, 'authority' is guaranteed by the 'absolute value' inherent in literature:

> there is as much stability in aesthetic judgements as in ethical or political or philosophical or scientific; [and] the reputations of poets and artists are not less but more assured than those of biologists or statesmen or metaphysicians.[65]

He then asks 'how should one recognise authority?' and answers that 'degrees only prove knowledge; look among those who really love art and literature', and he goes on to conclude: 'The artist, if he really is an artist, possesses absolute value which he cannot lose: the man of science, once refuted or superseded, retains no absolute but only an historical importance.'[66]

The moral authority invested in English literature was not simply 'eternal', it was also resolutely national. Perhaps this was best articulated in the course of the presidential address to the Association by Sidney Lee in 1918. Lee, a key figure not only within the Association since its foundation, but also with the *Dictionary of National Biography* from its earliest days, referred to the aims of the English Association, suggesting 'that English be the constant, the unresting ally and companion of whatever other studies the call of national enlightenment and national efficiency may prescribe'.[67] Some members of the Association hoped that English in education would help achieve such ends by addressing itself to countering linguistic perversion. S. K. Ratcliffe referred in 1909 to the need for the 'preservation, or restoration, of spoken English under the present conditions of rapid degeneration'. He talked of the language going to pieces 'before our eyes'. especially under the influence of the 'debased dialect of the Cockney . . . which is spreading from our schools and training-colleges all over the country. In ten years' time the English language will not be worth speaking.'[68] A Mr Shawcross, chairman of the examination board of the NUT, offered a similar contribution: he spoke of the 'revolutionary change' in the teaching of English in elementary schools over the previous ten years, and he went on (in the words of the bulletin report) to give 'his experience of Manchester children under the old system':

> they could parse accurately and analyse poetry, but they spoke the perverted Lancashire dialect of the towns, had a narrow vocabulary, and could not understand diction . . . . The conditions of the children's home life tended to nullify the efforts of the teacher to instil a little culture. . . . It was even possible to get children in the slum districts of a great city to love such a poem as Wordsworth's 'Daffodils'. He wished to put in a plea for the teaching of pure poetry in the primary school. Get a child to love a poem; every word and phrase in it need not be understood at first. The understanding would develop as the child grew older, and a clearer explanation could be given than was possible in earlier years.[69]

Arthur Acland, the then president of the Association, had already stated in his address to this meeting that in the promotion of 'effective use of the English language', one of the best means was 'to foster a love of English literature'.[70] Thus, English literature was seen by members of the Association as the most effective vehicle for establishing through elementary education acceptable standards of linguistic usage. The goal was to implant 'standard' English forms (linguistic and cultural) by inculcating a 'love' of literature (the most that might be hoped for in the elementary sector).[71] Within the higher sectors (preparatory, secondary, grammar, and public schools, as well as colleges of various kinds) the aim was much broader. This involved, at the very least, the nullification of any middle-class 'hatred' for learning, and for its replacement by a taste for the finer stuff of literature, and even, more ambitiously, a 'quickening' of the whole spiritual nature.[72] This strategy of inculcation and for more explicit interventions into the flow of subjective responses, experiences, and pleasures, had a great deal in common with the programme for a renewed Liberalism being developed at this time by L. T. Hobhouse:

> The heart of Liberalism is the understanding that progress is not a matter of mechanical contrivance, but of the liberation

of living spiritual energy. Good mechanism is that which provides the channels wherein such energy can flow un-impeded, unobstructed by its own exuberance of output, vivifying the social structure, expanding and enobling the life of the mind.[73]

Returning to Acland's presidential address of 1909, it is notable that he resumed exactly these themes, but now applied to English literature. One of the best means of promoting effective use of the English language, he claimed, was to foster a love of English literature. This could be achieved by removing all 'deadening and mechanical influences' thereby inducing 'a hope that the movement [centred upon the English Associ-ation] would penetrate the homes of the future'. 'Unless the love of literature was developed in the home, little progress would be made,' he concluded.[74]

At its most ambitious and sophisticated this strategy aimed at bringing the raw subjectivity of the student or pupil into palpable contact with that very stuff of life considered to inhere within the 'sacred' text. This goal had important consequences for the role given, not only to critical and scholarly commen-taries and other incrustations upon the essential text, but also to the teacher: 'In dealing with literature in any full sense, to efface oneself, to stand away, between the child and literature, is the highest and not the easiest of duties which the teacher can undertake.'[75] Walter Raleigh, Merton Professor of English Language and Literature at Oxford, also emphasized this negative role for the intermediary between text and reader when he warned of the dangers of any 'immodesty' on the part of the teacher. Teachers of literature must avoid any attempt to become 'living representatives of all the mighty dead'. Instead they must facilitate the proper mode of encounter between reader and text, that of 'falling in love'.[76] The pleasures of experiencing literature – that 'joyous thing'[77] – were intended to elevate the student into an affective domain where they might be imbued with a higher moral tone. As an ultimate, a more elevated sense of 'good form' or 'style' might be attained.[78] None the less, some statements by members of the Association reveal that the effacement required by this procedure was no more than a tactical ploy, since one of the dominant assump-tions of moral education was 'that morality was to be made a conscious aim of the teacher, but concealed from the pupils, who were to imbibe the influence from literature as habit or experience'.[79]

Conclusions

I have argued that the movement mobilized within and by the English Association drew its energy and force from the apparent capacity of 'English' as a novel cultural form to resolve a number of problems posed for the functioning of national institutions between 1880 and 1920. In one sense, there can be no doubt that success was achieved, if this is measured in terms of the degree to which the new English came to be established as the core of the modern curriculum at almost all levels of the national education system from the 1920s; indeed, this is the sort of conclusion that most previous histories of English have encouraged. But since the object of the present cultural history is not simply to plot, from within, the development of an academic discipline, it is necessary to assess successes and failures from a different standpoint.

The greatest success which flowed from the movement for the advancement of English in this period was in its effects within the professional classes and middle classes as a whole, where the new cutural and pedagogic form prepared the ground for, and subsequently helped to sustain, a renewal of modes of public communication (especially within broadcasting, journalism, the cinema, and publicity). But as a mobilizing centre addressing the whole nation, the success of English was never other than partial. None the less, in terms of public administration – of the building of administrative layers at sensitive points between the official state and the generalized public – the new English came to occupy a strategically important role. This was notable within the national education system where, from the 1920s, the ensemble of pedagogic practices and knowledges began to be reordered around a 'modern' curriculum centred upon English. This was in marked contrast to the situation in some other European countries where more formally theoretical disciplines came to be placed at the curricular core of the nation. In Britain, however, English has functioned to provide a substitute for any 'theory' of the national life in the form of an imponderable base from which the quality of the national life can be assessed. While it has never resolved long-standing tensions between discourses on 'culture', 'science', 'philanthropy' (later transmuted to 'welfare'), and 'national efficiency' (later, 'wealth creation'), it has provided a cultural domain apparently immune to the ravages caused by their continuing conflicts. The sense of 'Englishness' that English came to signify was apparently so free of any narrow patriotism or overtly nationalist or imperialist politics that any debate about the meaning of the term itself was deemed unnecessary until quite recently.

2

English, the state,
and cultural policy

I have shown how the new and relatively autonomous movement for the installation of English as a central mechanism for
general education became strengthened within civil society;
and furthermore how it built sufficiently strong links with the
official state for its leaders to offer the service of the movement
for the joint promotion of English as a cultural instrument of
the nation-state. In consequence, the Board of Education
appointed a committee consisting largely of English Association
members to investigate and report on the possibility of practical
steps in this direction. This committee produced the Newbolt
Report in 1921. On the basis of its deliberations the Committee
proposed a strategy for national cultural renewal by means of a
system of education led by the universities, and with English as
the central pedagogic instrument for the gaining of nationally
valuable experience.

However, responses to Newbolt were to become the focus of
the first major ideological rift within the class-based cultural
movement, a rift which was to undermine the strategy proposed
in the Report and usher in an era in which English would be
constituted in much more limited cultural terms. This chapter
is therefore an account of a *failure* to link English with national
policy, a failure which also resulted in a radical diminution of
the future influence of the English Association.

Since the Newbolt Report is the first, and indeed has

remained the single most comprehensive official report on English, there has been a tendency to use it as the key to the most fundamental ideological impulses of the discipline. The Report has been seen as providing the most authoritative collective manifesto for English ever issued.[1] Equally the Report has been read as revealing the essential features of English studies as a discipline.[2] The relationship between the Report and the new discipline is, however, historically more complex than either of these viewpoints suggests. Thus, it is not my object here to provide some heretofore unrevealed final 'true reading' of this text, but rather to understand its discursive organization as a specific set of responses to concrete historical pressures.[3]

In the context of the history of English studies, the Report can best be understood as an attempt to develop a strategy which would effectively link state concerns with those of a wider movement within civil society. In an address to the English Association, Henry Newbolt had himself expressed his antipathy to institutions of any kind (see p. 32),[4] yet both Newbolt and the Association played a crucial role in the preparation of this government report. Indeed, one way of viewing the Newbolt Report is as the outcome of a bestowal by the state upon a civil association of the right to report and make recommendations on public policy. Furthermore, the Report represents a familiar tactic through which influential groups are recruited in the voluntary service of state interests and policies. It is with this conception of the Newbolt Committee in mind that I now wish to examine their Report as a statement of cultural policy in the guise of a proposal for meeting educational requirements by merely technical means.

No less than in the case of arts policy, the relation between English and public policy is a matter of cultural politics.[5] Indeed, the history of public policy on arts, and of the Arts Council of Great Britain, offers real insight into the politics of English in education. In both cases the combined efforts of state functionaries, professionals, and selected volunteers from the 'community' were instrumental in shaping quasi-state institutions (often called 'quasi-autonomous, non-governmental organizations', or 'quangos').[6] Furthermore, a discourse on 'art' was a central factor for the work of the Newbolt Committee in their attempt to formulate a strategy for national cultural unity. Finally, it is notable that the moment of the Newbolt Report is also that of the establishment of the University Grants Committee as the quango for university education. If the foundation of the UGC stands as an attempt to relate narrowly-based civil institutions to the concerns of public policy and national agency,[7] the proposals contained in the Newbolt Report represent an attempt to provide for English a similar link with national policy. One other feature of the use of the quango for the administration of cultural policy should be noted since it bears closely on the cultural significance of Newbolt. This is the quango's apparent insulation of spheres of cultural policy and administration from two perceived 'dangers': on the one side freedom from the danger of state control can be claimed; while, on the other, democratic accountability and involvement can be avoided.[8] As will be seen, the Newbolt Report attempts to construct a similar status for English: as 'art' it will be said to transcend narrow state or class interests; while, as 'education' its function will be to refuse and actively combat the influence of majority cultures rather than be democratically responsible to them. Indeed, such a 'quasi-autonomous' status for English in education makes a good deal of sense when the wider strategic and social context of the Report is taken into account.

Plans for setting up the Newbolt Committee were initiated in the course of an unprecedented mobilization of the whole population to sustain what has been described as the first 'total' war effort.[9] This required the active incorporation of the mass of the population to serve the nation, at the expense of many lives, and it was a process which necessarily involved cultural as well as military and civilian social administration to an extent which survived the ending of the war.[10] Indeed, A. J. P. Taylor has argued that after 1918 'concern for the condition of the masses became the dominant theme of domestic politics'.[11] Educational policies were not immune from this tendency in their concern with the proper constituents of a national education system, which while serving to weld the nation into a coherent unit, would not disturb fundamental economic relations. It should be noted that the members of the Newbolt Committee, like other influential educationists such as Ernest Barker, were concerned not just about the working class, but also with the middle class, and particularly the salaried workers whose numbers were increasing so dramatically after the war.[12] It was on the basis of such national concerns that the Committee attempted to construct a version of English which while serving the state in strategic, institutional, and cultural terms, would also appear free from state control because apparently grounded in free individual identity.

Education and the nation

The influence of these broad parameters makes itself felt in the opening pages of the Report, to the extent that the Committee is prepared to revise its very terms of reference in the light of its wider concerns. They immediately outline a strategy for national cultural unity which requires the linking of discourses on 'education' and 'the nation'. This in turn necessitates an altered conception of 'education' itself:

> The inadequate conception of the teaching of English in this country is not a separate defect which can be separately remedied. It is due to a more far-reaching failure – the failure to conceive the full meaning and possibilities of national education as a whole, and that failure again is due to a misunderstanding of the educational values to be found in the different regions of mental activity, and especially to an underestimate of the importance of the English language and literature.[13]

Already the proposed new conception of national education has been linked to the teaching of English, which tends to suggest a degree of consonance and an elimination of any distinction between them. In fact, English turns out to overwhelm the very concept of education itself in that the overall goal is to provide 'the best use of English as a means of intercourse and of education' (1/5). This is by no means a minor point since, as will be shown below, the Report sets out a programme for cultural renewal which has implications well beyond the institutional boundaries of formal education. And, crucial to the direction in which the Report develops is the claim that both education and English should be properly conceived as offering guidance in the gaining of experience; experience (as will be seen) which provides a necessary foundation for the development of a free humane identity both at the level of the individual and of society. The successful transfer of such experience from teacher to pupil is taken to require a sense of a 'community of interest' which 'would be felt instinctively and immediately by the pupil':

> The most valuable for all purposes are those experiences of human relations which are gained by contact with human beings. This contact may take place in the intercourse of the classroom, the playground, the home and the outer world, or solely in the inner world of thought and feeling, through the personal records of action and experience known to us under the form of literature. (4/8)

In subsequent sections of the Report it becomes increasingly evident that, with the single exception of literature, all of these sources of experience are to be considered as potentially corrupting. Somewhat paradoxically, however, the Committee deplores the actual gulf which separates education from life. One tactic of the Report is to transcend this paradox by recourse to particular appropriations of the deceptively simple terms 'experience' and 'life'. This is achieved by treating highly selective versions of experience and life as if they covered the whole range of experiential processes and forms of living, which, in fact, excludes the normal experiences and lives of the vast majority of the population. The same applies to the Committee's use of the term 'reality' which, when placed in significant opposition to 'convention', refers back to the same selective cultural parameters. The point of this exercise is to limit the terms experience, life, and reality in such a manner as to enable the claim that popular access to all three can only be gained by means of art which, for the purposes of national education effectively means English and especially English literature.

The Committee's discussion of art is placed in the context of another significant opposition within the Report, that between the 'English mind' and 'the public mind'

> English is not merely the medium of our thought, it is the very stuff and process of it. It is itself the English mind, the element in which we live and work. In its full sense it connotes not merely an acquaintance with a certain number of terms, or the power of spelling these terms without gross mistakes. It

connotes the discovery of the world by the first and most direct way open to us, and the discovery of ourselves in our native environment. (14/20)

Set beside this, the public mind is indeed impoverished:

We find that the nature of art and its relation to human life and welfare is not sufficiently understood or appreciated in this country. The prevalence of a low view of art, and especially the art of literature has been a main cause of our defective conception of national education. Hitherto literature has . . . suffered in the public mind both misunderstanding and degradation. (14/20–1)

The notion of art upon which the Report draws is at once so general as to be almost unspecifiable, and so pragmatic as to offer a highly potent means of making practical and discursive links between English and education: 'The writing of English is essentially an art, and the effect of English literature in education is the effect of an art upon the development of human character' (14/20). English literature, as the art most readily available for education, is seen also as a means of encouraging goodness and strengthening the will, a central factor given the 'vast importance to a nation of moral training' (9/5).

The Committee considers that 'true education' is most readily and completely available through the works of English literature, while also emphasizing its difference from mere 'book learning': 'Books are not things in themselves, they are merely the instruments through which we hear the voices of those who have known life better than ourselves' (11/16–17). Furthermore, since 'the common unaided senses of man are not equal to the realisation of the world', education should provide the means by which the 'dull superficial sight of the multitude' can be 'illuminated and helped to penetrate in the direction of reality' (11/17).

It should be noted that the domain of 'reality' to which the Report here refers is taken to encompass both the essence of true English cultural and racial identity and true humanity. In this manner the discourse of the Report seeks to constitute a sense of 'English' which is concordant with all that is considered culturally desirable, valuable, and authentic, both from the point of view of society and of the individual. While the Introduction has little to say on language specifically, what is said conforms to this broad sense of English. Language in general is understood as communication and thought, command over which must 'take precedence over all other branches of learning'. However, an important distinction is inserted here between

> the language properly conceived, and perverse forms of speech and thought: among the vast mass of the population, it is certain that if a child is not learning good English, he is learning bad English, and probably bad habits of thought; and some of the mischief done may never afterwards be undone. (6/10)

Quickly, though, the Report moves to a much broader and more flexible conception of 'English':

> It is probable that no one would be found to dissent from this proposition [the fundamental importance of the teaching of the English language], in which the meaning of the word English is limited to the language itself as a means of communication. The word, however, in our present enquiry, has other and wider meanings, and these must now be brought into consideration. (7/10)

It soon becomes evident that these other and wider meanings cluster around a specific conception of the national culture. Thus, the Report refers to 'English in the highest sense' as 'the channel for formative culture for all English people, and the medium of the creative art by which all English writers of distinction, whether poets, historians, philosophers, or men of science, have secured for us the power of realising some part of their own experience of life' (8/12). There follows a passage in which the extended metaphor of free liberating and fertilizing flow situates English literature as the natural and unpolluted source for the most valid native experience and sense of identity:

> We are driven, then, in our search for the experience to be found in great art, to enquire whether there is available any similar and sufficient channel of supply which is within reach of all without distinction. We feel that, for an Englishman, to ask this question is at the same time to answer it. To every child in this country, there is one language with which he

must necessarily be familiar, and by that, and by that alone he has the power of drawing directly from one of the great literatures of the world. Moreover, if we explore the course of English literature, if we consider from what source its stream has sprung, by what tributaries it has been fed, and with how rich and full a current it has come down to us, we shall see that it has other advantages not to be found elsewhere. There are mingled in it, as only in the greatest of rivers could be mingled, the fertilising influences flowing down from many countries and from many ages of history. Yet all these have been subdued to form a stream native to our own soil. The flood of diverse human experience which it brings down to our own life and time is in no sense or degree foreign to us, but has become the native experience of men of our own race and culture. (8/13–14)

But those fertile cultural fields which are said to have been generated and sustained by this vitalizing flow of truly native experience turn out to be presently inhabited only by a 'limited section' of the society (10/15). The 'experience of men of our race and culture' in fact stands for the quite narrow culture of which the Report itself forms a part. It is a remarkable feat of cultural self-assertion to claim that such a culture could be taken to, and disseminated among the 'multitudes', a feat which only the buoyant sense of the self-evident value of imperial colonization could sustain. As we shall see, however, this sense of cultural vitality later comes to be severely inhibited by fears of social instability. This is registered in part by a shift from metaphors of natural flow to metaphors of invasion (see p. 62).

For the the moment the writers of the Report consider their educational programme of cultural diffusion by means of English to be 'in no way impossible or visionary':

an education of this kind is the greatest benefit which could be conferred upon any citizen of a great state, and . . . the common right to it, the common discipline and enjoyment of it, the common possession of the tastes and associations connected with it, would form a new element of national unity, linking together the mental life of all classes by experiences which have hitherto been the privilege of a limited section. (10/15)

The 'nation' referred to here is one within which social divisions are seen as having purely 'accidental and conventional' causes (15/21-2). Thus it is outside the power of industry and commerce to offer a remedy. Although 'commercial enterprise may have a legitimate and desirable object ... that object cannot claim to be the satisfaction of any of the three great national affections – the love of truth, the love of beauty, and the love of righteousness' (14/21). As will become clear, this claim is crucial to the development of the Report's strategy, given that the rise of modern industrial society is taken to be a major progenitor of contemporary 'accidental and conventional' social and cultural divisions. Indeed, it is from this base that the Report goes on to conclude that only the state, in its cultural and even spiritual manifestation, is capable of overcoming the forces making for national disunity.

Despite such transmutations, the task of spiritualizing institutions of state power did not prove to be easy. None the less, the Committee considered that the instruments were available and the time ripe for achieving this enormous ambition: 'We have the advantage given us by the necessity of a new departure among rapidly changing conditions, and by the opportunity of avoiding some causes of past failure' (10/15). The post-war world seemed ready for new institutional initiatives of cultural 'extension' drawing equally on the spiritual forces of art in the form of English, and established traditions of extended state and voluntary public activities.

As to the first of these, the Report simply endorses Board of Education thinking on the educational value of English, and more particularly English literary *works* (16/24). Like the unimpeded flow of the 'native' culture, the spiritual greatness of the literary work is incontestable: 'the greater the work the more clearly it speaks for itself' (16/24); 'even the teacher of English must bow before the experience of those great minds with which the works offer contact. This would allow a "bond of sympathy" between members of society to be subjectively sealed' (11/15). And, as to institutional extensions, the culminating sentences of the Introduction propose appropriate measures of action: 'The enrolment of a fraternity of itinerant preachers on English literature . . . would be a step in accord with other movements of the time and with our national tradition of unpaid public service' (17/25). In fact, the final sentence articulates the crucial link between public policy, national unity, cultural extension, and the systematic mobilization of these public servants:

> Nothing would, in our belief, conduce more to the unity and harmony of the nation than a public policy directed to the provision of equal intellectual opportunities for all, and service to this end would be doubly effective if it came voluntarily as from those who have already received their inheritance, and desire to share with the rest of their country-men that in which their life and freedom most truly consist. (17/26)

When formulated as 'conclusions and recommendations' these measures are all reduced to two policy planks, one for 'our' education and the other for English:

1 That our national education needs to be perfected by being scientifically reformulated as a universal, reasonable, and liberal process of development.
2 That for such an Education, the only basis possible is English. (348)

In reading the body of the Report it is clear that such a 'refounding' will involve establishing a programme for 'raising the mass' of the 'general population' (17/25). While this is undoubtedly a cultural policy and programme which is in-tended to administer to 'national unity', it is dressed up as a scientific and national response to established 'educational' needs.

Similarly, the term 'English' is not as inert or technically neutral as it appears in the recommendations. The specific educational practices proposed as 'English' within the body of the Introduction consist of systematic training in first, correct pronunciation and clear articulation in the sounded speech of Standard English; second, clear and correct oral expression and writing in Standard English; and third, reading aloud, reading for access to information, and – especially – reading for literary experience (13/19). Of course no explicit justifications for choosing such criteria of correctness are stated other than the supposedly inherent qualities flowing from a 'native' linguistic and literary tradition. The English which is to be formulated as the major instrument for achieving the more general policy goals turns out to consist of systematic inculcation of linguistic practices, firmly aligned to a very specific sense of Englishness. Within this programme, what appears in the formal recommendations as an academic or school subject, in fact consists of approved principles and methods for cultural intervention into popular linguistic practices with the overall purpose of generating a subjective attachment to a particular sense of national identity.

'Historical retrospect'

The centrality for the Committee's conception of English of a particular vision of national identity, is underlined in the following chapter of the Report. No conclusions or recommendations arise directly from this chapter, as is indeed appropriate for a section which purports simply to offer an objective historical narrative. Within the overall discursive architecture of the Report this narrative functions as the cultural–historical foundation for qualitative judgements of standards of correctness, and for a perception of contemporary cultural crisis.

The Committee begins by expressing surprise that the position of English within the educational system has 'scarcely any history' (18/27). However, such a revelation could only be surprising in the light of the Committee's own characterization of 'English' as a discipline of education, dependent in itself upon quite recent social developments (see pp. 44–5). However, rather than seeing 'English' as this recently invented pedagogic and academic regime, the Committee seeks to constitute recent developments as a simple extension to a much longer national history. Indeed, their very syntax encodes English as a self-motivating agent within a historical progression from language to literature: 'by the end of the fourteenth century the English language had definitely asserted itself against the results of the Norman Conquest and later French influences'. No longer a mixture of local dialects, Standard English 'had emerged', and the east Midland dialect 'had now become' the King's English; finally, 'through the works of Chaucer it became the literary language of the country' (20/28).

During the fifteenth and sixteenth centuries, the humanist 'revolution' in educational ideas led to a privileging of classical literature as the means of providing a liberal education, although this was later considerably transformed into a narrow disciplinary process tied to the maintenance of social distinctions. With the increase in population from the early nineteenth century, education in this illiberal form was unable to adapt itself 'to the needs of the new body of persons who turned to it for help' (41/42). The consequence was 'chaos' resulting from 'the absence of any broad general basis of education, such as English offers' (42/43), and from the lack of an English 'compactly enough built to do well in the scramble' (54/53).

Thus, the whole thrust (of what in fact is a much more extended 'retrospect' than indicated in this summary) is towards the construction of English as a sufficiently compact cultural instrument with which to refound the system of education:

> It will be noted that in these remarks we have given to 'English' a very wide significance. We have looked upon it almost as convertible with thought, of which we have called it the very stuff and process. We have treated it as a subject, but at the same time a method, the principal method whereby education may achieve its ultimate aim of giving a wide outlook on life. When that aim is kept in view, it will be found that English as a subject should occupy not any place which may happen to be vacant, but the first place; and that English as a method must have entry everywhere. (57/56)

National needs

A recurring theme within the Report is the inadequacy of any utilitarian or vocational form of education to the task of reconciling educational policy with what is perceived as the national interest. Within the discourse of the Report, utilitarian and vocational education are seen not only as inadequate vehicles for the effective 'cultural nationalization' of the working and lower middle classes, but also as positively dangerous to the extent that they generate unfulfilled cultural and economic expectations. In turning to the manner in which the Report deals specifically with the 'needs of business' it is immediately clear that the requirements of cultural nationalization are to be allowed completely to overwhelm the servicing of such needs. In fact, the Committee goes so far as to assert that business and industry have *no* distinctive educational needs, and is thereby able to collapse point 2 in its terms of reference ('the needs of business, the professions and the public services') into point 1 ('the requirements of a liberal education'). They conclude: '"the needs of business" are best met by a liberal education' (recommendation 30). The general force of the argument is to urge that the needs of employment, and employers, should influence as little as possible overall patterns of national education. Indeed, employers are urged not to interfere with the human being's 'stages of growth' and the requirements of 'an education appropriate to those stages' (137/133).

The incorporation of a long passage from a Board of Education memo on evening schools indicates that the Committee feels itself to be in consonance with the Board's thinking, not only on the inadequacies of vocational education, but also on the value of English as a force for cultural nationalization. Here 'English' is sufficiently broadly conceived to encompass 'the study of man' – as the Board's memo puts it (141/140) – or, in the Committee's own words, considered to be as 'wide as the English mind, and as broad as English life' (140/136). This is yet another presentation of English in education as the proper channel for transmitting the 'story of the English people'; in effect, an imaginative, or even imaginary mode of cultural or sociological study. This study has now been tied to a vision of Englishness which is itself insulated from any concern with cultural power and control.

A major feature of the Committee's (and indeed the Board of Education's) automatic correlation of 'English' with 'Englishness' is its provision for dealing with certain 'marginal' cultures. Thus, when drawing on evidence from Wales and Yorkshire which dealt with local as opposed to national forms (i.e. communal traditions of language and dialect, pride in place, manners and customs, speech, song and dance, acting, and craftsmanship), the Committee is able to find a place for them within their overall vision of Englishness, by saying: 'We believe it to be in the highest interests of English culture that local patriotism, with all that this entails, should be encouraged' (144/144–5). Given that 'local patriotism' could, and often did, entail active opposition to the Committee's sense of the English national culture, this statement, at first sight, seems odd within the overall discourse of the Report. However, as will be seen, this position is entirely in line with a view of Englishness which identifies it with a non-industrial or pre-industrial past. Given that it is a central goal of the Committee to encourage a public policy on education which will operate to generate and sustain an organic national culture, the only concrete examples within contemporary popular culture to which they can refer this policy in a favourable manner are those which are sufficiently residual as to be unable to offer more than a minimal oppositional purchase.

In the case of the majority popular culture which the Committee seeks to de-legitimize, the situation is seen very differently. Here the disjuncture between the culture of 'English' and the majority culture is presented in terms of a dangerous gulf between 'the mind of the poet, and that of the young wage-earner'. Here it is not a case of 'encouraging' local cultural development but of attempting to 'wean' people away from such influences as the 'cheap sensational periodicals' which are said to blunt their imagination, and – importantly – cause them to 'recoil from' and perhaps even 'come to dislike literature' (148/149–50). A serious issue indeed for the Committee given that literature is to be the central instrument for furthering its cultural programme.

It is clear that the Committee's project of combatting the 'diseased' majority cultures and sustaining a healthy sense of Englishness by mobilizing literature in education, has little place for serving industrial needs. Their sights are set elsewhere as is shown later when discussing 'some possible dangers in reading.' That this concern with 'dangers' is allied to a culturally interventionist stance rather than the service of pre-conceived needs is evident when they state that it will be their 'practical policy' to combat 'the dangers of print' which, while they 'cannot be eliminated, will be more and more easily repelled, as the germs of disease are repelled by vigorous health' (309/340).

The universities

The Report engages with policy for the universities in a more oblique and tentative manner than for schools or industrial and commercial needs. Despite the establishment of a quango for the universities, the extent of their 'national' role was still a matter of controversy, and for this reason discourses on the national education could not, without some difficulty, be made to coexist with those on the university curriculum. Thus, the Report considers the universities mainly in so far as their influence could be seen to be reflected back on the school system examinations and the home. While the university is taken to stand at 'the apex of the educational edifice' (190/195), its position there is sufficiently elevated to cause the writers of the Report to retreat (in this instance only) into a narrow conception of their frame of reference, thereby justifying a refusal to address the work of the universities as a whole. While 'the university is now immensely more important in the education of the nation than it used to be',

> with its work as a whole we are not here concerned. The duty of this Committee is confined to considering 'the position of English' in our whole educational system, which of course includes, and in our reference expressly stated to include its position at the Universities. (190/196–7)

The Committee's position on the nature of the English school within universities is entirely in line with this narrow viewpoint, and the same is true of their approach to examinations and research:

> It would be premature, and indeed impertinent, if we were to attempt to lay down in any detail the lines of a perfect 'School' of English. That is a problem for time, experience, and the experiments of many Universities to solve. (193/201)

> It is not our function to prescribe examination methods or standards to individual universities. (219/237)

> [Regarding the] differentiation between the various stages in the training for research work . . . on this matter again it is not our function to make detailed recommendations, but to lay down general principles. (220/239)

In this manner, the discourse of the Report affects simply to offer some general principles for the study and teaching of English. None the less, given the Committee's overall elevation of English, this discourse also implies a radical (if indirectly articulated) reappraisal of the university's role in society and of its curriculum. It is worth remembering this point when we come to consider some responses to the Report. It may be that responses from within the universities were shaped as much by an unwillingness to accept a national role for the universities, as by the Report's unprecedented prioritization of English studies.

In fact, the chapter on the universities concerns itself with uses of English well beyond the boundaries of the English school:

> English . . . is needed in every Faculty. It is the one subject which for an Englishman has the claim of universality. Without it he cannot attain to full powers either of learning or of teaching in any. We should like it to be officially proclaimed by each university that in all its examinations the quality of the English written or spoken by candidates, especially its lucidity and its fitness to the subject, will carry great weight with examiners. But this is far from all.

In fact the Report immediately makes clear the Committee's view that English involves far more than lucidity and fitness to a specific purpose, in that it is also potentially a powerful force for national cultural enrichment, and even international cultural ascendency:

> English is not merely an indispensable handmaid without whose assistance neither philosopher, nor chemist, nor classical scholar can do his work properly. It is one of the greatest subjects to which a university can call its students. Never was that more so than at this moment when English is nearer than ever before to becoming a universally known language . . . Most of this extension of English may be due to political or commercial reasons. But there are higher reasons

too. The intrinsic value of our literature is increasingly recognised . . . [Furthermore] no Englishman competent to judge doubts that our literature ranks among the two or three greatest in the world; or that it is quite arguable that, if not perhaps the finest, it is the richest of all. Such a possession, once recognised as it now is, no university can afford to neglect. (192/200)

At this point, however, the Committee is faced with the need to overcome a major obstacle to any general acceptance of the higher value of English in the university: the charge of being a 'soft option'.

This is an accusation which affects the whole of our enquiry. If it were made good, it would go a long way towards providing a justification for denying English the place in our educational system which we demand for it. Above all, it would be fatal to the claims of English at the University stage. (194/202–3)

The problem for the Committee here is that any adequate specification of the 'richness' or 'intrinsic value' of English upon which their claim for its 'greatness' as a subject rests, would require that these terms be subjected to a rigorous critical, historical, and sociological analysis. Such a course of action was rendered inconceivable by virtue of the Report's reliance upon a discourse on art to legitimize the centrality to be accorded English within the curriculum. In consequence, the Committee is forced back upon the classical model, despite the consistent tendency elsewhere in its pages to accord to English an educational validity independent from and at least equal to classics.

An Honours 'School' of English will at least start its candidates on a path which, if followed to the end, leads to such knowledge of English Literature as Bentley or Jebb possessed of Greek. No one who thinks for a moment will suppose that that is a path in which there are no hills to climb. It is clear, then, that the alarm of the 'soft option' may be dismissed as a bogey. (194/204)

When it comes to specifying the fundamental disciplinary components which constitute the actual means of engaging in this 'climb', the Committee selects exegesis, art, and history, while at the same time insisting that English literature should clearly be distinguished from history, and indeed sociology and philosophy (195/204–5).

It is interesting to note that, in attempting to refute the charge of 'soft option', the Report had already asked: 'Is it a soft option to make oneself master of the political philosophy of Burke?' (194/203). It is clearly implied that it is not. But, when to this implied answer is added the claim that literature stands 'utterly above any history' (195/205), a curious consequence follows. While philosophy and history may be used as part of a tactic for establishing the disciplinary validity of English against the soft option charge, the essence of English is none the less taken to inhere in its 'nobler, more eternal and universal element', that very artistic quality which is said to transcend both the historical process and all systems of ideas:

> There is a sense – the most important of all – in which Homer and Dante and Milton, Aeschylus and Shakespeare are all of the same age or none. Great literature is only partly the reflection of a particular year or generation: it is also a timeless thing, which can never become old-fashioned or out of date, or depend for its importance upon historical considerations. What does so depend in any of the arts, whether sculpture or painting or poetry, is in truth not great at all. (195/205)

In bringing into play this powerful discourse on art and the 'eternal' qualities of the human spirit to justify the distinctiveness of English, the Report is able to recuperate the very history which it claims to transcend, by recourse to an essentialist and narrowly-based cultural history of the 'English people':

> The ideal 'School' of English literature will . . . not, for a moment, allow itself to be made into a mere branch of History. It may be true that the story of the English people is best seen in English literature, but English literature contains much more than the story of the English people. (195/205–6)

Of course, the use of a category such as 'the English people' requires some sense not only of what that phrase encompasses, but of what is necessarily excluded from it. As has already been shown the discourse of the Report excludes not only the majority contemporary culture, but also any sense of former cultural, political, or social conflicts and struggles. Instead a vision of fertile English culture is linked to human freedom and truth and placed in opposition to the narrowness of science and the idols of the market-place (202/217; 204/220).

In presenting English culture as a transcendental essence inhering within an 'organic' national language and a humanistic literary tradition, the goal was to establish for the study of English at the universities a status equivalent to Oxford's *Literae Humaniores*. This was important because the latter School was taken to represent the highest standards of humane scholarship. Furthermore, classical languages and literatures appeared to be insulated from any possibilities of social, historical, or cultural revaluation, since their very distance from contemporary culture gave them the appearance of unified, organic, and completed totalities. It is worth noting that it was not the Committee's objective to assert directly the primacy of English over classics, but instead to capture for their subject some of the cultural authority invested in classics for an altered social and educational purpose. It was not for English to supplant classics as a vehicle for elite socialization. Rather the Report sought to present English as the principal means whereby the universities might both engage in and direct a much wider mission of national cultural renewal.

The crucial point is that the English department was to be elevated, not so much by virtue of its importance within the institution, but because of the role it might be made to occupy in leading, co-ordinating, and sustaining extra-mural initiatives:

In view of the growth of the tutorial class movement and of adult education generally, which carries with it an increasing demand for courses in English literature, the influence and responsibilities of English departments at Universities, especially in the provinces, are likely to be extended considerably in the near future. If these responsibilities be shirked, valuable and important work will either be held up for want of teachers or fall into the hands of those ill qualified to deal with it . . . The point, however, we wish to make here is that, from whatever source the teachers are drawn, their work with adult students should be regarded as university work; the

Professor of English should make it part of his duties to keep in close touch with them, periodical meetings of the tutors and the Professor, for the interchange of ideas and the discussion of problems should be held – in short that the extension and tutorial classes should be regarded as an integral part of the English Department. (230/248–9)

It has been claimed above that the Report is best understood within more general extensions of state cultural policy and management in its concern with mobilizing public activists, within a tradition of voluntary action, to serve the 'community'. It can thus be seen that both in this chapter and in the closely related one on adult education which follows, the Report addresses English professors and teaching staff not so much as professionals but as responsible public figures; as socially-concerned part-time and even voluntary preachers functioning to disseminate a national culture. As the final paragraph of the Report's chapter on the universities makes clear, this 'mission' is seen as extending well beyond the boundaries of England.

Every university must, of course, consider its own needs and resources in making provision for its teaching of English. But it should bear in mind that the subject is one of particular national importance and that . . . what is wanted is organisation on a national scale. In any plans for future development of their English departments, university institutions should consider not only their particular or local requirements but the rapidly expanding place of English Studies in the life of this country and indeed of all parts of the English-speaking world. (231/251)

Educating the public mind

The term 'mission' is a precise one, especially in the light of a discursive shift which is evident from the very first lines of the chapter on adult education which follows:

We have called the University the apex of the educational edifice. From another point of view it may be called the inner shrine. But around the edifice lies what the mediaeval poet called the 'faire felde full of folke'. Few of the folk pass beyond the outer court of the temple, though all must travel among the highway of life's pilgrimage which runs up to and beyond it. What has English, and especially English literature, for the wayfaring man who misses the scholar's introduction? . . . It is a question, we believe, involving grave national issues, and we have given much anxious thought to it. (232/252)

Two points are worth noting here. First, the anxiety-ridden sense of a need for national unity which is ideologically central to the Report finds no place at all in the formal 'conclusions and recommendations'. Second, the extremities both of gloom and zeal are most manifest when the Committee considers adult education and, especially, working-class attitudes to literary education. Furthermore, the evocation of 'wayfaring' folk instead of the contemporary urban proletariat introduces into the discourse of the Report a sense of Englishness linked to a mythology of medieval organic ruralism. It is this mythology which is to offer a means of spiritualizing a policy of intervention into the disturbing cultures of modern industrial and commercial society.

However, as has already been mentioned, the task of spiritualizing a utilitarian state machine is no easy one. This explains the absence from the 'conclusions and recommendations' of any reference to national spiritual unity (or of contemporary challenges to such unity) given that in this section the discourse addresses itself to details of state policy. Much of the body of the Report, in contrast, takes the form of a discourse on the nation rather than the state; indeed, the opening section of the chapter currently under discussion is sub-titled 'Literature and the nation'. The goal is to construct a spiritual unity for the nation, of which the state policy is merely a neutral servant. In this way English, and especially English literature, can be established, not as a strategy for political and cultural intervention, but as a transcendence of political operations:

> For if literature be, as we believe . . . a fellowship which 'binds together by passion and knowledge the vast empire of human society, as it spreads over the whole earth, and over all time', then the nation of which a considerable portion rejects this means of grace, and despises this great spiritual influence, must assuredly be heading for disaster. (233/252–3)

English, like England, is presented within this discourse as essentially and incontrovertibly a matter of culture without politics, the self-evident and natural servant of a spiritual fellowship embodying all that is true, good, and free. This explains why the chapter on adult education is at once the most overtly political in its aims and the most transcendental in its language. It also explains its oscillation between a concern with shrines and pilgrimages, with sanctification and the Holy Ghost, with poetry and the human spirit, and – at the other pole – an anxious and gloomy preoccupation with class antagonism, and with the need to consummate new territorial invasions of dangerously uncolonized cultural spheres. The following passage crystallizes most of these concerns:

> We have a traditional culture, which comes down to us from the time of the Renaissance, and our literature, which is rich, draws its life-blood therefrom. But the enormous changes in the social life and industrial occupations of the vast majority of our people, changes begun in the sixteenth century and greatly accentuated by the so-called Industrial Revolution, have created a gulf between the world of poetry and that world of everyday life from which we receive our 'habitual impressions'. Here, we believe, lies the root cause of the indifference and hostility towards literature which is the disturbing feature of the situation, as we have explored it. Here too lies our hope; since the time cannot be far distant when the poet . . . will invade this vast new territory and so once more bring sanctification and joy into the sphere of common life. (237/258)

It is at the same time stressed, however, that it is not the 'true function of literature' to engage with the contemporary 'social problem'. Instead, while literature 'contributes no specific solution to the social problem it endows the mind with power and sanity' (235/255). The function for English preferred by the Committee, then, is one of aligning the popular imagination and culture (what is elsewhere called 'the public mind' (see p. 46)) with a sense of communal identity having sufficient 'sanity' to neutralize not only 'the hostility towards "the culture of capitalism" now prevalent in Bolshevist Russia' (235/254), but indeed that antagonism and contempt for literature which is said to be found among 'the working classes, especially those belonging to organised labour movements' (233/252).

National intellectuals

It is, of course, clear that the Report does not speak on behalf of working-class culture, but it should also be noted that it distances itself from the culture of the middle class (cf. 236/256–7). Instead, the Report offers a discourse which both addresses and speaks on behalf of what may strictly be identified as 'national intellectuals'. This is the group to whom the writers of the Report themselves belong, as indeed do most of the policy and decision makers active within the state apparatuses and its quasi-autonomous and semi-voluntary extensions, especially within the field of education. Not only does the Report address this group, it attempts to consolidate conditions for their functioning as national intellectuals, and to enhance their sense of identity.

This offer of a spiritual identity was considerably enriched through its association with a potent instrument for popular cultural intervention. Their own educational socialization primarily through classics could not adequately have equipped them for the task of the 'total' administration of a national culture. Indeed, if anything, it had insulated them from urban industrial life. Now they were being offered as the basis for policy, a suitably tailored 'native language' which could be understood as the only common cultural resource of the whole nation, and administered as such. However, the role played by literature in tailoring this common resource meant that it was 'common' only in a highly idiosyncratic sense. According to the mythic cultural history which contributes so much to the discursive architecture of the Report, the 'native language' only achieved cultural maturity through its spontaneous generation of literary art. Thus, 'English culture' could be taken to have been shaped, at least in pre-industrial times, equally by artists and community. While it was obviously impossible to claim that literary art still sprang from the general community, this could be accounted for by the gulf between literature and life caused by the processes of industrialization. Literary art could then be presented as the only means of determining the properly national cultural qualities within a divided society; a literary art which was the province of the poet rather than the state or any ruling class or group. In fact it is the absence of any territorial invasion by the poet into contemporary culture, which authorizes certain interim measures overseen by the state on behalf of the nation.

Within such a discourse national intellectuals need not see themselves as attempting to impose their own culture orientations upon a majority population. They need not conceive of their practical programme as one of systematic cultural intervention: they were simply making transitional preparations for a reincarnation of the spirit of Poetry:

> the time cannot be far distant when the poet . . . will invade this vast new territory, and so once more bring sanctification into the sphere of common life. It is not in man to hasten this consummation. The wind bloweth where it listeth. All we can do here is to draw attention to the existing divorce, and to suggest measures that may lead to reunion. The interim, we feel, belongs chiefly to the professors of English literature. (237–8/258–9)

The passage which follows has commonly been taken as providing a basis for subsequent conceptions of the role and function of professional English teaching. In the context of the Report as a whole, however, it should be understood instead as a call for a systematic strategy of cultural extension by extra-mural means addressed primarily to an adult population, rather than as an internal tactic for English as a discipline.

> The rise of modern Universities has accredited an ambassador of poetry to every important capital of industrialism in the country, and upon his shoulders rests a responsibility greater we think than is as yet generally recognised. The Professor of Literature in a University should be – and sometimes is, as we gladly recognise – a missionary in a more real and active sense than any of his colleagues. He has obligations not merely to the students who come to him to read for a degree, but still more towards the teeming population outside the University walls, most of whom have not so much as 'heard whether there be any Holy Ghost'. The fulfilment of these obligations means propaganda work,

organisation, and the building up of a staff of assistant missionaries. (238/259)

It has been suggested that this restates Arnold's conception of a group of 'apostles of culture' who disseminate the 'best' that is known and has been thought. In fact, the Report makes clear that it aims at much more. Its objective goes beyond the dissemination of knowledge in recommending an active and intimate engagement within popular subjectivities and forms of signification. The type of cultural intervention envisaged by the Committee involves not just a preaching mission, but also active cultural transformation of a kind which requires a certain degree of 'love', or a liberal and sympathetic attachment not only to 'folk' cultures but even to urban industrial cultures: 'The ambassadors of poetry must be humble, they must learn to call nothing common or unclean – not even the local dialect, the clatter of the factory, or the smoky pall of our industrial centres' (238/260). That there are severe limits to the extent to which such sympathy is to be extended need not be doubted given the Report's general refusal to positively evaluate any culture seen as untouched by literature. In these circumstances the only available solution is to find something 'poetical' even in the life of the 'common people' on the basis of which a sympathetic resonance with the literary tradition may be elicited. This point is made in the Report by quoting Henry Sidgwick's suggestions for propagating the 'noblest' culture and making it prevail:

> It can only propagate itself by shedding the light of its sympathy literally; by learning to love common people and common things, to feel common interests. Make people feel that their own poor life is ever so little, beautiful and poetical; then they will begin to turn and seek after the treasures of beauty and poetry outside and above it. (238/260)

When articulated as a teaching programme for English one of the most interesting features of this urge to develop a 'common touch', or an affective bond between teachers and taught, is the centrality to be accorded to popular tastes, however 'crude and unformed' they might be considered to be.

> the tutor must first of all explore the minds of his students, their tastes and prejudices, and build on these. To begin by

throwing the classics of English literature at their heads is generally to count failure. . . . The vital thing is to make it obvious from the outset that literature is alive, that it is the sublimation of human thought, passion, feeling, that it is concerned with issues which are of universal interest, that in short it is flesh and blood and not stucco ornamentation. (252/276)

In some sense this mental exploration can be seen as coextensive with the work of the other 'social explorers' who, continuing a tradition from Victorian times sought to investigate the 'dark continent' or 'jungles' of working-class life.[14] By the time of the Report such social exploration and documentation had become firmly linked to public policy and administration, especially in terms of a 'structure of feeling' which Raymond Williams has identified as 'social conscience'

> what has most carefully to be defined is the specific association of what are really quite unchanged class feelings – a persistent sense of a quite clear line between an upper and a lower class – with very strong and effective feelings of sympathy with the lower class as victims. Thus political action is directed towards systematic reform at a ruling-class level . . . It is a matter of social conscience to go on explaining and proposing, and at the same time help in organising and educating the victims.[15]

The unique contribution of the discourse of the Report to this 'social conscience' was its offer of English as the instrument of an affective strategy for educating the emotions of the 'victims' so that as individuals they might be raised spiritually above the mass while at the same time remaining excluded from political and economic power and the decision-making processes. It is this which marks the discourse of the Report as distinct from strategies for 'rational' public policy and social administration. The sympathetic link finally envisaged was between the individual subjectivities of members of the popular classes and an 'English culture' or national identity, to be achieved by English as a vehicle for state policy. As the final sentence of the chapter puts it,

The belief which inspires every paragraph of the present Report is that this much-desired spiritual unity in the nation and the equally necessary uplift in the whole level of the popular imagination can only come through a general acknowledgement of the paramount place which the native speech and literature should occupy in our schools and in the common life of our people. (252/277)

3
English as a masculine profession

It has been shown how the discourse of the Newbolt Report offered to universities a leadership role within an ambitious programme for intervention into popular cultures and literacies. The Committee's version of 'English' at university level was thus shaped according to the requirements of providing a centre of mobilization and a potent pedagogic instrument.

However, as responses such as George Gordon's suggest, there was little indication that university schools of English were willing to accept such an instrumental role and cultural identity simply to serve state policy.[1] During the inter-war period, the quasi-autonomous model of administration (the quango) was not yet geared to any effective imposition of a programme of this kind upon the universities, or the schools of English within them. As C. D. Burns remarked in 1924: 'We have . . . developed in England a compromise by means of which the educational system is in great part a State system and the standard of education is largely set by the universities free from state control.'[2] Thus, despite the formalization of a system of state subsidy with the foundation of the University Grants Committee, any fears that university autonomy might be lessened were considerably allayed by the known attitude of the President of the Board of Education, H. A. L. Fisher, enshrined in his dictum: 'The state is, in my opinion, not competent to direct the work of education and disinterested research which is carried on by the universities.'[3]

During the war, under Lloyd George, a policy had been pursued which combined vigorous prosecution of the war with all-round reconstruction on the home front. Within this context, education was to be given priority as the chief means 'for promoting in social life that equality of condition with which men now faced death on the battlefield.'[4] With Fisher's appointment as President of the Board (having a seat in the Cabinet) came an undertaking that money would be made available for such post-war reconstruction; and the policy itself was enshrined in legislation to enable the kind of educational expansion within the continuing and adult sectors which had been at the forefront of the Newbolt Committee's deliberations.[5] In practice, however, such expansion was never enacted, despite the ever-increasing reliance of the universities upon state funds (by 1931 they were receiving slightly over half their income from this source).[6]

So, while the universities were recognized as having a national role, it was not the one envisaged for them by the Newbolt Committee. Instead, their autonomy as centres of professional learning was enhanced, with only some small limitations. They were expected to recognize the national competitive importance of research and institutional efficiency, as formalized by the introduction of new postgraduate degrees (especially the Ph.D.), and by the standardization of their administrative, faculty, and departmental structures.[7]

In consequence, the identity of English studies during the inter-war period was forged, not out of the discourses of the Newbolt Report, but rather in terms of the subject's consolidation as an autonomous academic discipline and learned profession. Furthermore, in becoming fully inserted into the structures of university education, the distance of the discipline from schooling, state policy, continuing and adult education, and indeed lay literary culture, was progressively accentuated. By the time English had situated itself as a centre of learning and teaching at all universities in the early 1930s, its ethos and evaluative criteria were those associated with a masculine profession, rather than with a programme of national cultural intervention. As will be shown, in this period the community of feeling, aspiration, and practice, as well as the conditions for the reproduction of the discipline, involved the negotiation of a completely new set of pressures.

Of these, three should be mentioned here. In the first place it was necessary to establish and constantly confirm an appropriate canon and pantheon as the basis for scholarly work. Second, there was the need to construct a professional scholarly stance upon which to build modes of training consistent with the kinds of sensibility which would enable critical evaluation, not only of literature, but of fellow professionals. And, finally, the discipline was required to develop a distinctive orientation to, and difference from, lay literary cultures of high aestheticism, social poise, and hedonistic impressionism.

The major development during the inter-war period was the establishment of English studies as a bulwark against, rather than force for social change and cultural innovation. Instead of being guided by any ambition to oversee a national cultural mission, the disciplinary impulse was directed towards establishing English as a humane profession. Thus, inter-war English studies was devoted to professional scholarship, research, and publishing rather than a programme of cultural intervention. Work of the kind published in the *Review of English Studies* (henceforth *Review*) is more indicative of inter-war activities and attitudes than are the policies of the English Association, or indeed the *Scrutiny* movement. An analysis of the contents of the *Review* does indeed reveal a continuing concern with the national dimensions of language and literature. However, it is also clear that in the course of the inter-war period this concern came to be accommodated to such values as taste, tact, and decency that were characteristic of the male-focused professions.

The professions already provided broadly influential models of masculinity, especially within the middle class. 'The Professional Gentleman' embodied an ideal of unemotional, rational, 'asexual' maleness which was insulated against any tendencies towards emotional degeneration.[8] Characteristically within traditional professions such as Law and Medicine, it would have been beyond the bounds of decency to put any of one's peers or the profession itself in a morally ambiguous or cynical light. In English, a similar stance came to be taken, not only to fellow professionals, but to the great authors and their works. It is clear from the contributions to the *Review* discussed below, that within English as in the established professions, perceptions of individual worth became tied to professional stances, practices, and subjectivities.

Furthermore, the academic discipline of English studies followed the familiar dynamics of a professionalizing process in which the conditions of being human were themselves masculinized. Masculinization of social institutions is of course not necessarily displayed as overt sexism or discrimination. For example, women were not excluded from the discipline, particularly as students. In fact they were allowed some professional space (albeit not specifically 'as women') to engage in scholarly work on the 'man to man' discourse with which the field was largely concerned. Although overt proclamations of the need to maintain English as a 'manly' educational pursuit by no means disappeared during the inter-war period,[9] the pages of the *Review* reveal few of the defensive and often hysterical avowals of the discipline's 'manliness' that had been characteristic of the earlier period. As Hearn has remarked: 'Where masculinity is secure, it need not be strenuously affirmed.'[10] In practice during the inter-war period English was (and largely remains) securely established as a stable and male-dominated professional field despite the presence of a majority of female students.

In the event, the masculine qualities associated with classical studies when channelled into English provided a most effective antidote to the traditional female associations of literature.[11] The professional ideal for the discipline was constituted as the achievement of a complete 'personality'; a quality and character understood to be inalienable, and therefore immune from the mutabilities of style, manner, vocabulary, and imagery. As will be seen, literature and the discipline which was based upon it were seen primarily as a means of transmitting personalities, on the model of the *Dictionary of National Biography*. Despite disclaimers which recommended submission to great works, the professional study of English came to transcend even the literary masterpieces themselves by virtue of its capacity to offer a complete and final assessment and achieve the kind of complete historical understanding unavailable to the historical actors themselves.

As the detailed analysis of the contents of the *Review* given below clearly reveals, inter-war English studies attempted to offer the literary work, and the cultural continuum within which it was placed, as a palpable experience of the harmonious fusion of diverse influences beyond all actual social divisions. The study of English seemed to provide direct access to an apparently historical but in fact imaginary world in which a uniform English national character was fully harmonized with unique individual diversity and independence. If the 'polite society' of the eighteenth century most frequently provided a historical simulacrum of this harmonious world, literary fictions were presented equally as harmoniously unified texts which guaranteed this reality within the boundaries of taste and tact. Furthermore, English studies, as an aesthetic discipline which channelled access to the writer's experience as an artist, seemed to offer a spectacle of the ineffable in which value that was at once human, English, and literary simply exhibited itself prior to any rational explanation.

But with this dream of harmony came its own nightmare world. However professional and manly and disciplined the stance taken on their subject matter, English academics continued to be worried by their inability to account rationally for the intrinsic value, style, spirit, and mood of the literary work. Thus, the discipline remained dogged by the problem of accounting for literary value despite its professional insulation from exposure to the danger of degradations of value in the extra-academic worlds of the literary market-place, the school system, and mass culture.

The *Review of English Studies*

Founded in 1925, the *Review* is in many respects a source as appropriate to this phase as the English Association and the Newbolt Committee were for the earlier period. From its first issue it identified itself as a co-ordinating centre for research in English studies, and indeed, the development of an identity based upon research for the discipline can be seen to have been one of its major functions. Though published quarterly, it was very different from the traditional quarterly literary journal. Certainly, from the beginning there were clear links with extra-academic initiatives, especially in publishing: its editor for the whole of this period, R. B. McKerrow, was a partner in the publishing firm of Sidgwick & Jackson rather than an academic.[12] It was only at the end of McKerrow's long tenure in 1940 that the *Review* was taken over by the Oxford University Press. The personnel of its advisory panel[13] is indicative of the subsequent irrelevance of disputes about the Newbolt Report for subsequent developments within academic English. Newbolt himself was there, as were some other former members of that Committee and some of its major critics. The panel also included a sprinkling of other non-academics, but such extra-academic connections were to prove increasingly tenuous, as was the degree of the *Review*'s continuity with the discourses of the Newbolt Report and issues of public policy.

The *Review* usually contained about four articles (seventy-two pages), 'Notes and Observations' (about three pages), and about forty-four pages of reviews. Only very occasionally were editorials carried, and other miscellaneous contents included short notices, lists of books received, obituaries, and at the end of each year a 'roll of honour' listing all successful English graduates by institution and name. In the early years pamphlets were reviewed from time to time, but this practice was soon discontinued. In fact, it is probably accurate to understand this as one feature by which the mode of publication previously very characteristic of the English Association, can be differentiated from the professional journalism of the discipline in its newer, more autonomous academic guise.

It would be difficult to reduce the contents of the *Review* over this whole range to some kind of collective ideological manifesto, but for reasons different from those discussed above in relation to the Newbolt Report. The very few editorials included were largely confined to discussing technical matters of scholarship, and the *Review* did not, in general, speak out directly on wider cultural–political issues. In the main, therefore, its ideologies are to be found in the form of its embodied working practices and unquestioned assumptions rather than at the level of manifest policy statements. Its collective identity (perhaps like that of English studies itself) was structured into its range and mode of cultural production and enunciation.

Language and cultural policy

The progressive disengagement from extra-academic concerns, particularly at the level of cultural policy, is best revealed by the *Review*'s approach over this whole period to the study of language. At first, discussions of language provided the predominant occasions for considering wider cultural relations and policies as well as narrow technical issues. In its early days, a contributor like Allen Mawer could use the occasion of a review of Jesperson (who was concerned with 'conservative' definitions and redefinitions of grammar) to refer to wider social issues.

And interestingly, one review by Mawer contains the only mention of the Newbolt Report to be included in the *Review* during the whole of the inter-war period, and this solely in the context of attributing to the Report responsibility for generating a good deal of subsequent discussion of grammar.[14] It is worth noting here that first, it is through an emphasis on language that the only direct links are made with the work of the Committee, and second, reviews of works on language are the only ones which attend to textbooks in schools rather than in universities. Indeed, every issue of the *Review* contains the statement that 'As a general rule no textbook below University standard can be noticed.'

The special, if residual, connection between language and the cultural strategy of the Newbolt Report is further clarified in an article by J. H. G. Grattan, 'On the Anglo-American cultivation of Standard English'.[15] Here it becomes clear what is at stake in developing a grammar which will provide acceptable criteria for distinguishing 'right' from 'wrong' in linguistic usage: intervention into the culture of the masses. Since writing in English is

> no longer confined to persons who speak the King's English or who come under the direct influence of the great writers; the continuity of our literary and linguistic heritage is threatened by the far-reaching influence of the half-educated ... We must give up regarding 'good English' as merely a social or literary accomplishment, and ... endeavour by research and by exposition to equip the masses with the ability to exercise a reasoned choice in the employment of language; in other words ... we must regard the

training of the linguistic consciousness as an essential part of primary and secondary as well as University education.[16]

The occasion for this article was an inaugural meeting in June 1927 of the International Council of English, held under the auspices of the Royal Society of Literature, and involving both American and British scholars. The involvement of Americans is significant in that Grattan sees it as important to learn from their country's experience of conquering linguistic 'barbarism' within 'her vast alien immigrant population'.[17] This places his discourse firmly in the domain of public cultural policy and returns us directly to the concerns of the Newbolt Committee, indeed to one of its major areas of anxiety: 'Whether the class-consciousness which has hitherto formed the chief force of [linguistic] stability in Great Britain, will continue to influence the masses, has yet to be seen.'[18]

However, the *Review* was never again to engage directly with these issues after 1931. By the end of the inter-war period, a very different relationship to conceptions of 'language' had been forged within the *Review*'s pages. In the course of the 1930s language was increasingly considered only in relation to the literary work, no longer to social and cultural policy; a transition seen most notably in the reception given to the writings of F. W. Bateson (see p. 90). Spoken English was to be of less and less concern to the *Review*, while 'literary language', and especially that of fellow professionals, came to be a constant preoccupation, especially in the book review pages, where any lapses from 'intelligibility' were regularly and severely censured. In sum, the academic English scholar was becoming less of a public policy maker in aspiration, and more of an arbiter and custodian both of literary language and literary knowledge.

The discourse of 'art'

Another strand which had fed into the cultural policy making of the Newbolt Committee emerges in an altered form within the *Review*. In the Report 'art' had been used to legitimate a realm of cultural value in such a manner as to render it equally immune from state interference and democratic accountability. The strategy had been to mobilize this vision of art by means of the missionary work of national (as opposed to state) intellectuals. In contrast, within the *Review* little recourse is made to a discourse on art except in relation to the poet's or writer's *activity*. The focus here is more upon the literary work itself and the 'experience' of the writer which is invested in it, and 'art' in this case is that which is manifested in unique and harmonious literary works, a harmonious fusion of diverse influences.[19] This is entirely appropriate to a form of academic work which spent much effort in locating and charting such diverse elements as well as increasingly concerning itself with the principles of their harmonious unification within the text.[20] In fact, both the diversity of influences and their fusion through the writer's activity provide constant discursive themes for contributors to the *Review*. Herbert Grierson, reviewing a book on Swinburne,[21] writes of the value and pleasure to be gained from studying the development of a 'great poet's art' in all its phases. 'Art' here signifies the artistry with which the writer transforms available influences and finds an appropriate form of unified expression. The scholar is expected to analyse the artist's 'thought and sensibility', the passing phases of 'style' in the formative period, and the influences which 'coloured the artist's work in passing', especially 'if in the end that art achieved complete independence and individuality'.

Art is approached through a sense of the writer's individuality and independence as taken to be expressed in poetic, and increasingly prose works. However, contributors to the *Review* were largely unwilling to go so far as to attempt to specify the nature of artistic quality in general, despite the fact that their own capacity to decide which texts were of sufficient interest in themselves to justify study depended upon recognizing such quality.[22] It is usually assumed that the ineffable in art is beyond the province of the professional academic scholar. Edith J. Morley, for instance, writes of the 'inexplicable value' of great poetry, and advances the view that such poetry 'can explain itself only "by existing" so that in one sense every attempt at an explanation, however worthwhile, is doomed in advance to failure, or, at best, only partial success'.[23]

None the less, the sense of a need to provide some kind of discourse on literary quality is evident from the earliest issues of the journal. There are a number of attempts to 'estimate more surely the intrinsic value of the work' by finding the means to capture its 'spirit and mood'.[24] In a similar vein, there are references to a 'new spirit' which is said to have raised 'the standard of literature and taste' in the eighteenth century,[25] and to the need to attend to 'particular aspects' of the writer's achievement.[26] It seems clear that writers for the *Review* felt the need to bring, in Marie St Clare Byrne's words, 'something real into the nightmare world where "stylistic" evidence flourishes'.[27]

Such efforts to engage with discourses on quality by means of notions like 'taste' and 'style' may be understood in terms of challenges issuing from the peripheries of the discipline, as well as beyond its boundaries, which called upon the leaders of English studies to provide an account of 'literary quality' of at least equal force to those being generated outside the *Review*'s pages. While Byrne considered that Caroline Spurgeon's 'imagery analysis' offered a way out of the stylistic nightmare,[28] critics of the English 'establishment' were not so impressed, as Francis Mulhern has noted:

> *Scrutiny*'s earliest and most protracted campaign was against the positivism of traditional literary scholarship. The 'value-free' assumptions of conventional academic research were repeatedly challenged by the journal's reviewers, and its conclusions dismissed as inadequate, conformist or simply worthless. Caroline Spurgeon's analyses of Shakespeare's imagery were met with suspicion by R. G. Cox, who insisted that there would be 'no substitute for literary criticism'.[29]

A humane profession

For the most part, though, the *Review* concerned itself more with establishing for English studies a status similar to that of the humanism of classical studies, than with criticism. The range of humane and other qualities most admired is best illustrated by the contents of the few obituaries carried in its pages. William Archer, for example, is remembered for that 'sane and instructed judgement' which 'did much to recover English drama for literature from triviality'.[30] As the obituary for Israel Gollancz shows, such 'sanity' when applied to disciplinary practice, involves skilled exposition, and interest in 'the work in

hand' rather than in literary criticism.[31] It is equally illumin-
ating to examine what counts as 'solid achievement' for writers
in the *Review*. Gollancz, for example, is commended not only for
his qualities as a teacher, but also for his contributions to the
development of institutions such as the British Academy, the
Shakespeare Association, and the Early English Texts
Society.[32] Similarly, C. H. Herford, in addition to being described as 'the most accomplished English scholar of his age', is
praised for his institutional contribution as 'the successful head
of the great school of English at Manchester'.[33] But most
interesting of all is the treatment given to Sidney Lee, described
in his obituary as biographer, Professor of English, writer on the
place of English literature in the modern university, and for
thirty years editor of the *Dictionary of National Biography*.[34] In
reviewing Lee's work, Ernest A. Baker identifies him as the
complete 'humanist' by virtue of his classical scholarship, his
faith in beauty and reason, and his exalted hopes of human
progress. He is a complete 'personality', and comparable therefore to those other 'personalities' whose 'transmission' has been
the function of the *Dictionary of National Biography*. Living persons are not fitted for such transmission, and even the dead must
be guaranteed by their 'solid achievement' (political, literary,
military, or other). On occasion (most notably in the case of Dr
Johnson), 'fine personality may be an achievement in itself'.[35]

A consistent emphasis on character, personality, and integrity is to be found within the pages of the *Review*. Much more
energy is expended on providing admirable examples, and
springing to the defence of those whose integrity is threatened,
than to the elaboration of literary-critical judgements. For
example, when comparing Swift to Shaw, the former's 'vastly
sounder humanity' is unproblematically asserted by Oliver
Elton.[36] Elsewhere, 'accusations' and 'charges' against Milton
are refuted,[37] the degree and nature of Macaulay's 'sincerity' is
defended,[38] 'worthy and good-natured mediocrities' are
dismissed,[39] and Arnold is rebuked for his 'petulant
snobbishness'.[40] There are three important consequences resulting from this concern with transmitting and protecting the
'humanity' and 'personality' of great authors. First, textual
effects are given only secondary importance: 'style, manner,
vocabulary and imagery may be borrowed, but personality is

inalienable'.[41] Second, any true scholar is expected to have a capacity to respond to – and indeed share in – these humane qualities. And finally, the professional 'student' of English is actually elevated above authors, at least to the extent that hindsight (like death) enables not only the making of a complete and final assessment, but also the development of a historical understanding which was beyond the comprehension of the historical actors themselves. As McKerrow put it: 'much of what we strive to find out was not and could not be known to those of the period which we study, for it was veiled from them by the life of everyday.'[42]

Professional specialization

Increasingly in the course of the inter-war period work carried out by the *Review* tends towards the production of extremely specialized and exclusively academic scholarship. It is interesting to note that earlier in the period the work of non-academic scholars (such as the civil servant E. K. Chambers) plays an important role within the *Review*. In 1931, Charles J. Sisson, writing of the 'solid foundation' for Shakespeare scholarship laid by Chambers, A. W. Pollard, and W. W. Greg, remarks that,

> It is a matter of pride to us that we can boast of several scholars, in the first rank, who are not university teachers. None rejoice more in this leaven than the professional scholars themselves. It seems to be a feature almost peculiar to this country, and nothing could be healthier for scholarship.[43]

However, by 1940 the purely professional academic character of the discipline is much more marked. In that year the editor is to be found wondering 'whether the fate of "English Studies" will not eventually be smothered in a kind of woolly and impenetrable fog of wordiness that few or none will be bothered to penetrate'. He is forced to accept, however, that by this stage, most of the readers of the published articles read them 'out of a sense of duty' and 'a wish to keep up with what is being done,' rather than 'because they have any real interest in the subject'.[44] This trend to professional academic specialization is confirmed by G. B. Harrison, writing in 1940 on the *Review*'s first fifteen years: 'It will hardly be denied by anyone who looks through the files of the *Review* that the earlier numbers were more interesting than the later', which he put down to the 'increasing specialization in English, as in all forms of study'.[45]

Within this transition, there seem to have been two distinct phases of development, the second of which was ushered in with the final abandonment of all residual concerns with cultural and linguistic policy, and thus indirectly with English in schools. Some remarks made by P. Gurrey in 1931 can serve as an indicator of the closure of the first phase. Referring to the by now well-established consensus that grammar should be based upon 'educated' usage rather than some abstract principle of 'correctness', Gurrey is none the less unconvinced that any radical change is likely to take place given 'the inability of the leaders of today to learn, and their intellectual self-sufficiency'.[46] In fact, such intellectual self-sufficiency had by then come to characterize English itself as an academic discipline. In future the pages of the *Review* would carry no further discussion of such general social–cultural issues, and Gurrey himself later took such concerns away from academic English studies and into the school sector.[47]

The encounter with modernism

The intellectual self-sufficiency of the discipline also extended to its attitudes towards contemporary literary production. By the early 1930s the terms 'modernism' and 'modernist' had begun to appear occasionally in the review pages, signalling an at least minimal engagement with contemporary literature, particularly poetry. However, viewed from outside, the increasing insulation of academic English from the lay literary world might well appear to its discredit. Certainly this is at the root of what Stephen Potter considered to be the 'dispiriting preconceptions' with which academic English shackled the literary muse.[48]

Such criticisms were launched not only from outside university English. By the mid 1930s internal factions had gathered around the journal *Scrutiny* in a systematic opposition to the dominant trends represented by the *Review*. According to the former, English studies was seen as failing to hold true to its proper identity as an educational principle and cultured force. The *Review*'s response to this challenge was an oblique one. Within the review sections attempts began to be made to develop a discourse that was at once professionally autonomous and modernizing, critical as well as scholarly. This did not, however, involve offering the voice of *Scrutiny* a place within the *Review*'s discursive ensemble: no publication by the Leavises, Richards, Empson, or any other of the Cambridge 'revolutionaries' was ever reviewed between the wars.

The relationship between the *Review* and *Scrutiny* is best seen within the context of the general reception given in the former journal to modernism, and especially to T. S. Eliot. From 1930 some tentative engagement with the difficulties and aims of the modern poet can be found in the review sections.[49] (None the less, it should be noted that a critical essay of Eliot's was dismissed because it said 'nothing new' three years later.)[50] A. C. Ward, reviewing a book called *The Trend of Modern Poetry* in 1936, notes the impossibility of achieving 'neutrality in the face of the conflict between right and left groups in contemporary poetry', and therefore applauds attempts to 'bring the apparently isolated modernists into the main traditional stream of English poetry'.[51] The introduction of F. W. Bateson as a regular reviewer from this same issue marks a more consistent and considered attempt at a settlement with modernist literature and criticism. Bateson's own work had been favourably reviewed in 1930 for its combination of research with wit, wisdom, and style.[52] Given his scholarly credentials as a researcher, Bateson, when introduced as a regular reviewer, was in a strong position to deflect attempts to 'discredit' the 'Eliot school' of poetry, by drawing on contemporary critical work such as that of Empson to explain the new poetry's layers of intelligibility and ambiguity.[53]

Bateson recommended, for example, that the sources of modern poets such as Auden should have the same scholarly apparatus applied to them as used for (say) Spencer, so long as Auden's sources were investigated 'with at least as much thoroughness and intelligence as Spencer's receive'.[54]

The process of settling accounts with modernism, as with the new emphasis on poetic value, can thus be seen as a serious if limited one. In fact it was not finally completed within English until the post-war period, with Bateson once again a prominent influence. To understand the terms in which this settlement was progressively forged it is necessary to consider the major critical and scholarly strategies of the *Review of English Studies* as a whole, of which this incipient settlement was only a small feature.

The Review*'s overall project: a spiritual continuum*

The major focus at all times within the *Review* is upon the completion of the historical map of English literature, thereby conserving and protecting its professional plenitude. The project's main aims and objects are set out in an editorial by R. B. McKerrow carried in the first issue.[55] The *Review* is to be devoted to research 'in all departments of its subject'. Such research provides the 'lifeblood of literary history' as long as the focus is on 'new facts' and 'new relations between the old'. The process of interpretation requires the amassing of information about 'great contemporaries, their lives and their writings'. If we look also at the review sections, we see that already in the 1920s McKerrow takes the view that a 'great period of discovery' is rapidly coming to an end: 'an age of English scholarship is passing, if not already passed'. Scholars can now be considered fortunate if they manage to find 'one unworked field'.[56] Three years later, McKerrow describes this great period as constituting a 'revolution in literary history' in the course of which everything previously taken as axiomatic has been questioned or disproved. He says that a new generation of students has been considering the '"facts"' that remain from a very different angle. In place of the nineteenth-century sense of a succession of literary historical 'periods', scholars have now revealed a continuum of 'interlocking elements' making it clear that in all times the 'spirit of literature' is one.[57]

Another early contributor, A. W. Reed, sees it as the task of research to illuminate this spirit:

> Literature is illuminated rather than obscured as we come nearer the personality and circumstances of the writer; and provided that at all times our aim is to illuminate literature, we are on the side of the angels. Biography, bibliography and

philology wait in attendance on literary appreciation; these four together cover the whole field of literary research.[58]

At this early stage in the period the spiritual continuity of the field is seen as guaranteed by its pastness and completeness. Scholarship involves attempting to remove all obscurities so as to come as close as possible to this essence. The technical goal is the construction of a critical apparatus which will not upset the underlying harmonious unity of the field, but simply authenticate the available empirical facts and ensure that they are correctly grouped and placed in proper relationship with each other.

The character of the underlying essence is made clear in H. C. Wyld's account of 'Layamon as an English poet': revealing the harmonious identity between human character, literary quality, and a culture of Englishness. Even though there is in Layamon's *Brut* no expression of 'religious belief' or 'moral intention', there can be no doubt that 'the writer is a man of a high and generous nature, with a true reverence for whatsoever things are lovely and of good report, and rich in every human quality which goes to make a man and a poet'.[59] For Wyld, *Brut* exhibits the kind of genuine human feeling which bespeaks a true 'poetical' intention on the writer's part by using a language which is 'not merely the ancient speech of Englishmen' but is also in true succession 'to the old poets of his land', and thus to 'the essential genius of the race'.[60]

Three years later, Edith J. Morley commends Oliver Elton for his 'emphatic' claim that 'our early poetry' mirrors the 'English genius', and that there is 'a true continuity of spirit, as well as of expression, in our poetry'.[61] Elsewhere, Morley commends those critical qualities of 'sanity and reasonableness' which, without recourse to any 'fireworks or display', ensure that 'the unbroken line of development in English literature is . . . convincingly exhibited to the unbeliever.'[62]

By the mid 1930s the sense of this spiritual continuum had been established as the fundamental precondition underlying all professional work of the kind represented in the *Review*. Englishness, as a sense of racial or spiritual identity, had come to function as a stabilizing force within the field of professional English studies, rather than providing the authority for a programme of cultural intervention. By the end of the decade, this Englishness was sufficiently pervasive to imbue both Anglo-Saxon writings and the novel equally:

> Everything is already unmistakably English. This mere Englishness is usually called Romanticism by those who do not know Anglo-Saxon.[63]

> The English novel, like the English character, is marked by independence and individuality. It cannot, save by strain and artifice, be divided into aesthetic segments or schools of thought.[64]

Disciplinary conservation

However, this apparently self-confirming synthesis appeared to be endangered by excessively specialized work, and even by some of the discursive themes through which the professional distance of the discipline from cultural policy and mobilization had itself previously been confirmed. The varying attractions of discourses on 'science' is a case in point. In the first issue, as has already been mentioned, McKerrow places a strong emphasis on 'facts'. At the same time, he distinguishes the procedures of literary history from those of the 'natural sciences'.[65] Ifor Evans, writing a few issues later, goes much further: 'if aesthetic criticism is to become a reputable study, as honest and sober as philology, it must develop a method and vocabulary as precise and exacting as those of the physical sciences', so as to be able 'to describe with an almost mathematical rigidity the content of a poetic creation or an aesthetic theory'.[66] And indeed, in his eyes this seems possible:

> There would appear to be no valid reason why poetic achievement should not be analysed by philosophical or even psychological methods. But the critic who undertakes such a task becomes a scientist, and he must shut out the ornaments of speech and persuasive language of the impressionist as dangerous guests in the laboratory of literary dissection.[67]

Approaches seeming to have a scientific basis are often welcomed by contributors to the *Review*. F. E. Hutchinson wishes to see scholars using 'a thoroughly careful *apparatus criticus* of the text'.[68] N. R. Tempest welcomes work involving the 'scientific analysis' of imagery, words, thought patterns, rhythm, tone patterns, and visual devices.[69] However, from 1934 claims for poetry's transcendence of science begin to find their way into the review sections (for example, science is seen as limited to 'the analytic faculty', while poetry involves the 'instinctive apprehension of the whole').[70] By 1940 McKerrow himself is said to have come to oppose 'pseudo-scientific' methods.[71]

In considering the period overall, it must be concluded that the pervasive professional discourses within the pages of the *Review* were not those of science but of Parliament and the Law, and even Medicine. One of the most admired scholars for the *Review*'s contributors is E. K. Chambers, and the terms in which he, and his work, are praised clearly reveal shared assumptions regarding desirable professional attributes. Charles J. Sisson praises Chambers for the comprehensiveness of his collection of 'instances', but also for his 'notable unwillingness to hasten to theory'.[72] The admired qualities are those, not of the theoretical scientist, but of the conservative and supposedly disinterested professional:

> Sir Edmund, in fact, belongs to no School of theory or of experiment, but preserves an independent, if sometimes apparently capricious, judgement against all tides, with a conservative bias. Like the House of Lords, he acts as a brake upon what some may call intrepid progress, and others think foolhardy innovation.[73]

This allies closely with the contemporary conception of the professions as among the most stable elements in society; A. M. Carr-Saunders and P. A. Wilson (*The Professions* (1933)) consider that the professions

> inherit, preserve and pass on a tradition ... they engender modes of life, habits of thought and standards of judgement which render them centres of resistance to crude forces which threaten steady and peaceful evolution ... The family, the church, and the universities, certain associations of intellectuals, and above all the great professions, stand like rocks against which the waves raised by these forces beat in vain.[74]

There is plenty of evidence in the *Review* that taking a professional stance of this kind helped sustain the discursive architecture of English studies in the inter-war period, especially in taking the disputative and judgemental stance of Parliament and the Law and borrowing the language from those discourses. H. Granville-Barker, reviewing Chambers's work, recognizes both the limitations of 'science' ('no art lends itself wholly to scientific methods of criticism and research') and the 'magnanimity of true learning' which 'scorns special pleading, comes charily to conclusions, opens every path by which the reader may reach his own'.[75] Another contributor considers that the 'proofs' gained from 'careful sifting and weighing of evidence' enable a judgement as to whether or not the scholar is faced with 'a capital crime'.[76] Reviewers even posture at once as barrister and judge:

> This concludes the evidence. We have examined Lord Lumley . . . but he has so far not only failed to prove a single alibi, [also] on cross-examination his case would seem to have completely broken down. Is he guilty or not guilty?[77]

The impulse to acquit Milton of 'charges' and 'accusations' has already been mentioned.[78] But there are many other instances where contributors take an adversarial stance against fellow reviewers ('I submit that it is fatal to his case'),[79] or one of advocacy on behalf of favoured authors (Pope is 'cleared entirely of a number of grave charges').[80]

In general, then, the discursive trend is towards establishing approved modes of argument and debate according to Parliamentary and legal criteria rather than submission to the rigours of the scientific proof. Furthermore, such modes of discussion are expected to conform also to the rules of professional *literary* discourse. Failures to conform in this way are adjudged by the journal's reviewers to provide evidence of a scholarly inadequacy which is taken to reflect a personal lack of taste and tact. Thus, much is made of the need to eliminate 'blots' on scholarship such as grammatical slips, errors in construction, 'tricks' of inversion.[81] Techniques of scholarly investigation, and particularly modes of 'literary' exposition and expression are tied to perceptions of individual worth, in a manner also quite characteristic of other professions.[82] The degree of 'humanity' to be attributed to professional colleagues is closely linked to the 'taste and tact' exhibited in their scholarship. Vivian de Sola Pinto sums up the qualities required of this kind of professional scholar as a capacity for 'exact scholarship', an extensive 'knowledge' of language and literature, and – if possible – 'the most perfect taste and tact'.[83]

The limits of decency

Apart from the threats posed to the spiritual continuum, and the discourse on professional humane scholarship by excessive specialization, certain other tendencies could serve to undermine the synthetic unity of inter-war English studies. In the final analysis, neither specialization, nor 'crude and slovenly workmanship',[84] nor technical inadequacies, were seen as the greatest dangers. The real challenge was as much moral as technical.

The nature of this challenge emerges, for example, when Mabel Day warns against any 'cynical treatment' which would deprive the literary work of 'much of its moral appeal'.[85] Most undermining of all is any stance which goes even beyond such 'cynicism' and 'passes the limits of decency' – however scholarly the technical procedures may be. Duncan C. Macgregor clearly delineates the boundary beyond which scholarship must not go, in his review of William York Tindall's book on Bunyan.[86] While recognizing Tindall as a 'diligent student', and even 'capable researcher', the work is 'vitiated . . . by the author's frankly avowed purpose in writing it'; his claim, that is, that Bunyan's writings owe their nature to the social, economic, and sectarian conditions of the author, and the literary conventions of a 'company of mechanicks'. It is this 'odd prejudice against his subject' which causes Tindall to move beyond the bounds of 'decency': 'What are we to say of a research student who . . . [sets] in an ambiguous light the author of one of the greatest books in our language, and one of the greatest religious forces in the life of England?' The only answer given to this question is to evoke the collective opinion of Macaulay, Froude, and Mark Rutherford: 'One wonders', writes Macgregor, 'what these men would have thought, and said, about Mr. Tindall.'

By the end of the period, the professional values of English studies had been rendered synonymous not only with the central moral force of the 'national character' but also with the moral worthiness of the scholar–critic (living or dead). A threat to any one of these is therefore perceived as threatening the others. By the same token, any discourse which seems to offer a synthesis between professional values and a sense of national character and moral worthiness, while also overlooking inhumane specialist tendencies and threats of moral ambiguity, is treated favourably in the *Review*. Louis B. Wright's *Middle-Class Culture in Elizabethan England* is welcomed by C. Bowie Millican on the grounds that it confirms a healthy trend in literary research whereby antiquarian, statistical, and editorial work are made to contribute to a broader and more comprehensive 'cultural synthesis': 'it is the proper evaluation of such information . . . that leads to perspective and reveals literature to be both a continuum and a truthful mirror of life.'[87] Similarly, C. S. Lewis's *The Allegory of Love* is praised by Kathleen Tillotson for charting the nature and evolution of two 'principles', or fundamental movements of the human mind – romantic love and allegory: 'It is rarely that we meet with a work of literary criticism of such manifest and general importance as this.'[88]

However, any generalist discourse deemed to be insufficiently 'discriminating', such as sociology, is banished from the field of English studies: 'Literary history here is strictly a branch of sociology. The novels considered are those read by the undiscriminating crowd.'[89] Of course, one of the grounds upon which the *Scrutiny* group claimed superiority to the English establishment was their capacity to provide a discourse which could link 'discrimination' to a 'literary sociology' through a close analysis of the language of literary, and other, texts. Within the *Review*, which was the scholarly organ of this establishment, the capacity to make value discriminations was assumed to arise from the 'taste and tact' associated with gentlemanly breeding, fortified by 'zeal, devotion and learning'[90] rather than 'critical ingenuity'.[91] In contrast to this, the voice of *Scrutiny* represented a new *petit-bourgeois* presence within professional English studies whose source of cultural authority derived, not from gentlemanly taste and tact, but from the pulse of their own sensibility; from their 'intelligent' and 'discriminating' capacity to 'enforce' their value judgements.[92]

Francis Mulhern[93] has argued that *Scrutiny* developed and propagated for the profession of English studies an ideological framework suited to the maintenance of a *talent*-governed career structure which eventually came to dominate the profession as a whole. The 'Scrutineers' achieved this in a number of ways. First, they attacked what they saw as the belles-lettrist and philological establishment within the discipline. Second, they offered a synoptic discourse within a singularly enfeebled and fragmented general intellectual culture. And, finally, they provided a charter and sense of function for *petit-bourgeois* professionals within the educational sphere, both at school and university levels.

Valuable as this account is, in its necessary emphasis on *Scrutiny* and Cambridge it tends to obscure a wider perspective covering the full range of cross-currents within English during the inter-war period. The 1920s and 1930s are just as notable for *resistance* to incursions from the peripheries of the discipline, as for the rise of *Scrutiny*. Nor was this resistance to diminish in the post-war period, as will be seen in the next chapter. The whole process of incorporation of the *Scrutiny* discourse within English was perhaps more contradictory than Mulhern suggests. Even before the war, Cambridge English itself was split between 'fairly incompatible traditions' including intellectual history and moral thought and the critical study of major works.[94] In fact, despite the common characterization of Cambridge as the home of the Eliot–Richards–Leavis modernist and New Critical 'revolution', it is noteworthy that T. R. Henn, a prominent member of the English faculty, referred in 1933 to 'the vulgarity of most of Eliot's work, all the more pernicious since cloaked by an austere and pseudo-learned style', comments which would have rested easily in the review section of the *Review of English Studies*. And furthermore, F. L. Lucas (librarian of King's) would not even allow Eliot's work to be bought for his library.[95] Lucas also took a view of the *Scrutiny* movement consistent with the *Review*'s general position on 'value judgements'. Writing in 1933, he describes the New Criticism as 'organised orgies of opinion'. For Lucas 'It is our business to see that those we teach have the knowledge and understanding without which judgements of literature are impossible; their judgements must remain their own affair.'[96]

None the less, within the *Review* itself a particular kind of space was offered to modernism, seen especially in reviews written by Bateson (see pp. 81–2). It is interesting to examine the conditions which allowed him to argue so positively in favour of modernism within the *Review*. Reviewing a book by Bateson in 1935, J. R. Sutherland considers that he has developed 'an approach to literary history that holds . . . much promise'. Bateson's work is seen as challenging a view of literature as the product of 'social forces' in favour of an analysis based upon the *language* poets had to use in any given period. This work holds out the promise of a much wider project:

> one wonders . . . whether the suggestions so originally and persuasively outlined here are capable of being worked out in detail by one man. If the linguistic side of our University Schools of English could be persuaded to give rather less of their attention to the roots of the English language and to devote more of it to the leaves it has put forth so abundantly since 1500 there would be far more data for literary scholars like Mr. Bateson to work upon. As things are, he has not only to invent his method, but also do most of the spadework for himself.[97]

It is clear that Bateson's emphasis on the continuity and relative autonomy of 'literary language' represented a modernizing position compatible with the sense of a cultural continuum which (as has been argued above) characterized the dominant paradigm within English studies. It was compatible also in that its procedures were much more closely aligned to historical scholarship than to critical evaluation, while at the same time enabling engagement in detailed analyses of literary language.

Conclusion

It is now possible to identify more easily the place of modernizing and modernist discourses within English studies of the second half of the 1930s. Francis Mulhern has noted the centrality during the 1930s of 'an intellectual culture led by publishing and associated lay activities'.[98] The prime means of intellectual organization was the periodical, overshadowed however by the massive shapes of Oxford and Cambridge.[99] It is not clear, though that the *Review* is best seen in terms of a 'regression towards the traditional pattern that still held in English Studies' as Mulhern elsewhere suggests.[100] Furthermore, the above account has indicated that the *Review* was not as 'devotedly philological' as characterized by Mulhern.[101] The *Review* always stood outside that lay literary world, or at least emphasized its academic distinction from it, and is in fact better seen as an enterprise typical of a new phase of academic English described by Gross in the following extract:

> By the 1920s a mood of sombre professionalism had set in, best exemplified by the founding of the *Review of English Studies* in 1925. The academic *apparatchicks* were in full command, and it was too late to change the pattern that had been laid down.[102]

It is clear that this 'mood' could only have come to dominate the study of English by deflecting the major challenges to its status as a 'real discipline'. This had involved countering charges of the discipline's 'effeminacy' as well as its associations with the lay literary world. Indeed, the achievement of a disciplinary identity based upon academic research had by the late 1930s more or less excluded the amateur scholar–gentleman. However, the 'sombre professionalism' or intellectual self-sufficiency of inter-war English studies had not been achieved without some breakdown of mutual comprehension within the discipline itself. Despite many attempts to establish acceptable modes of mutually intelligible professional literary language, such efforts had been undercut by increasing specialization and an at times impenetrable scholarly discourse.

Furthermore, despite their efforts at refuting 'charges against' the humanity and sincerity of their approved authors (and thereby by implication against themselves), scholars had never managed fully to provide any rational means for that complete assessment of personality which had been an object of all this effort. Certainly scientific approaches had come to be seen as unsuited to this project and therefore increasingly discarded.

Finally, much work of research and exposition during the

period had been devoted to an attempt to recover in full what each author meant through exhaustive biography, critical survey, and detailed examination of the author's particular achievement. However, the work of charting a trans-historical literary field, through the classification and interpretation of interrelated historical facts, perhaps represents the discipline's greatest inter-war success. The impulse here had been to establish as securely as possible the stability of the field by identifying an essential and continuous Englishness which was equally present in such disparate forms as Anglo-Saxon poetry and the modern novel. The discipline had thus successfully established and maintained the continuity of the English genius as an at once moral, human (i.e. ungendered), and poetic force; and it had developed procedures for regulating the admissibility of particular fictional works to this field of predominantly male-to-male discourse. But even here the discipline faced some problems. Since by the end of the period there appeared to be few unworked fields left within the discipline, its overall stability seemed endangered by excessively specialized work. This explains the welcome given to any cultural syntheses which might be expected to renew belief in the uniform spiritual essence both of English literature and of the discipline itself.

Both the current state of play within the discipline, and some indications as to future transformations, were given in an inaugural lecture by the new Professor of English Literature (G. L. Bickersteth) at Aberdeen on 12 October 1938 (the exact date is not without significance, as will be seen). Bickersteth was at pains to make clear that the time had come to discount 'scientific' discourses as offering an appropriate professional identity for English studies:

> despite the now fashionable equation of knowledge with 'science', the average undergraduate, whatever his special intellectual bent, still demanded that a university should primarily concern itself with giving him a liberal education.[103]

For Bickersteth, such a liberal education can be realized only through 'a first-hand acquaintance with the masterpieces of

English literature'.[104] This looks forward to a future phase of professionalism. Much more than in the *Review*, the concern here is with the quality of service offered to the 'client' or 'consumer'. As such, Bickersteth (following I. A. Richards) favours a literary pedagogy which offers to the student 'a unified state of consciousness' which is 'induced by the impression' received from 'the poem as a whole'.[105] The 'main purpose and aim of the study of English literature' is to build 'a constant habit of mind, since the mind when thus disposed, and only when thus disposed, can be truly described as liberally educated'.[106] However, 'for more than a generation' university schools of English have been dominated by 'historical critics' attempting the 'impossible' task of fully recovering 'the meaning imputed to a poem by the author and his contemporaries'. Against this Bickersteth argues for an academic emphasis on the 'living' meaning of literary works.[107] Thus the need for a revision of the scientific emphasis: 'the activities of the English department . . . make of it . . . a university in miniature, a school not of one but many sciences'. But the teacher of English knows that 'experience' has proved that 'science alone' will no longer suffice, especially in a world in which 'scarcely a fortnight ago it was only the imaginative vision of one wise man which saved mankind from the awful catastrophe that threatened them.'[108]

Despite such wise and imaginative intervention (by Neville Chamberlain) the catastrophic threat was, of course, soon to become a gruesome reality (the war broke out less than a year later). But even the new 'world-convulsion' did not impede attempts of this kind at building a new professional synthesis within English studies. If anything, the effort was accelerated – with significant consequences in the aftermath of the war. While most of the strands from which the new synthesis would be woven are already visible before the war, they could only be patterned into a new web within the altered conditions of the university in society, and in the 'national life' of the post-war era.

4
English, culture, and democracy

In the modern post-war period various adjustments within the national system of education have resulted in a succession of controversies regarding the role of English in a democratic society. From the 1940s many educationalists and university policy makers took the view that any modern democratic nation had to be a well-educated nation (or at least to have a well-educated intellectual class, and a revitalized bureaucracy). As a fully-masculinized professional field, the study of English increasingly came to be organized according to hierarchical administration, specialization, and approved modes of scholarship. However, under the pressures from institutional expansion and changes to the student constituency the internal discursive constitution of English was substantially altered, especially in the course of the 1960s. In this period the view of popular culture as degenerate and threatening came to be tempered by new pressures upon English academics to show that the discipline embodied a sense of social responsibility. However, this sense had now to be articulated in new ways. Criteria for student selection had become increasingly 'merit' based and the social constituency from which they were drawn widened slightly. Most important of all, the development of informal pedagogies, the sense of a need to combat the 'problems' of students' home background, and the perceived challenges from new youth cultures, resulted in the construction of a new agenda for staff/student communicative exchanges.

This was also at the root of altered perspectives on the cultural role of the discipline. Claims that English in education could offer some more or less democratic alternative to popular culture began to appear immediately after the war. At first contemporary 'mass' society was felt to be conformist, debased, and unimaginative. Thus, English academics came to present the discipline as uniquely suited to producing mature, free, and (in some instances) democratic men, on a model different to that of the inter-war gentleman of taste and tact. When in the 1960s English was subjected to the pressures of massive institutional change, the new model provided the context for a whole sequence of disciplinary disputes. Indeed, in the course of the latter decade the figure of the 'mature man' became increasingly discredited, or at least challenged as the appropriate basis for the discipline's cultural aims and functions.

This chapter concludes by examining the ways in which the notions of maturity and masculinity which had sustained professional links between English and Englishness were challenged from a range of pluralist, marxist, feminist, and other cultural perspectives during the 1970s, which, in the context of a counter assault from the new right, culminated in the symbolic 'Cambridge Crisis' of 1981.

English and 'culture'

The view that the universities should have a more central role in offering the kind of imaginative vision necessary to save 'mankind' from contemporary destructive forces was given an added impetus in the course of the Second World War. As has already been noted (pp. 92–3), Bickersteth had argued, even before the outbreak of the war, that English (if constituted as the university in miniature) was the academic discipline best suited to offer a degree of human wisdom appropriate to such a task. In fact, during the war years such views received their most consistent and sophisticated formulation in the pages of *Scrutiny*. F. R. Leavis gathered together his contributions to this discussion in *Education and the University*[1] which was published in 1943. This book, though most directly concerned with English studies, touched on many wider educational issues which were to become the subject of considerable debate after the war.

For Leavis, Cambridge English offers a way forward for the discipline as a whole by virtue of its emancipation from 'linguistic grinds' and Anglo-Saxon, but only on condition that it now becomes infused by a 'general discipline' addressed to the growth of 'intelligence and sensibility'.[2] It is clear that Leavis is less concerned with preserving the continuity of Englishness from Anglo-Saxon times to the present than with investing English with a new function, that of fostering within a class of disinterested intellectuals those qualities of wisdom called for by Bickersteth before the war. The strategy is to build upon, but also transform, the cultural authority long invested in the universities, by means of a wide pedagogic programme grounded in English literature. Rather than attempting to define the nature of the 'humane education' thus envisaged, Leavis merely asserts that 'It seems better simply to point to English literature, which is unquestionably and producibly "there", and to suggest that the "literary tradition" that this unquestionable existence justifies us in speaking of might . . . be called a vague concept.'[3] Of course, as has been shown, neither English nor humane education were simply 'there', but had been laboriously constructed over a long period. Leavis, however, professes to be unworried about any historical or conceptual vagueness, since he is more concerned to seize the opportunity and mobilize the symbolic force of 'cultural tradition' in order to 'check and control the blind drive onwards of material and mechanical development, with its human consequences'.[4]

This perspective is closer to that of the Newbolt Committee than to the guiding impulses of inter-war English studies. Indeed Leavis repudiates the latter as tending to

> foster a glib superficiality, a 'literary culture' too like that of those *millieux* of which the frequenters cultivate quickness in the uptake, knowingness about the latest market-quotations, and an impressive range of reference, all at the expense of real intelligence and disinterested understanding or interest in anything but kudos.[5]

At the same time, it is also clear that Leavis is not concerned with 'extending' English in the manner of Newbolt. What is essentially distinct from the Newbolt strategy is the altered relation to state and public policy. It is not Leavis's goal to produce 'national intellectuals' to serve as state missionaries, but rather a free-floating and critical educated class, membership of which is characterized by a particular kind of mental orientation: 'It is an intelligence so trained that is best fitted to develop into the central kind of mind, the co-ordinating consciousness, capable of performing the function assigned to the class of the educated.'[6] Professional intellectuals, so trained, could place the symbolic force of the university under the 'guidance' of a deeper 'inclusive and unifying purpose'.[7]

In contrast to the practical consciousness represented by the inter-war *Review of English Studies*, Leavis proposes a definite 'discipline' for English studies which is generalist, critical rather than empirical in orientation, and thus devoted to developing an intelligence and sensibility very different from that of the forensic lawyer–statesman. He calls for a reformed profession built around a new 'common enterprise' and involving 'wide active co-operation' among its members.[8] This enterprise is no longer to depend on discourses drawn from outside. Instead, it will possess a unique discourse of its own:

> The essential discipline of an English School is the literary-critical; it is a true discipline, only in an English School if anywhere will it be fostered, and it is irreplaceable. It trains, in a way no other discipline can, intelligence and sensibility together, cultivating a sensitiveness and precision of response and a delicate integrity of intelligence – intelligence that integrates as well as analyses and must have pertinacity and staying power as well as delicacy.[9]

Leavis does not question or problematize the existence of the materials of the literary tradition, and the moral force to be associated with the study of English resides, not in the 'personalities' of great authors, but in the capacity of an intellectual and professional elite to 'respond',[10] that is, to recreate in themselves that evaluative response to cultural change seen as inscribed within the literary tradition. The sense of continuity articulated here is very different from the pre-war 'continuum'. Underlying Leavis's reformed discourse on English is the sense that a major cultural transformation during the seventeenth century is at the root of the subsequent debasing modernizing process. The literary tradition is valued in so far as it offers a critical evaluation of this transformation and its consequences. This is why Leavis recommends that students be prescribed a piece of extended work dealing with the process of change by which 'the England of the seventeenth century' became the 'England of today'.[11] This piece of work should study 'in concrete terms' the relations between the economic, political, moral, spiritual, religious, and literary strands within English culture, attending particularly to such 'key-concepts' as order, community, civilization, and – most importantly – culture.[12]

In other words, Leavis is proposing that English be transformed into the study of *culture* based on 'a sense of the subtle ways in which, in a concrete cultural situation, the spiritual and the material are related'.[13] To this extent he can be seen as supporting a synthesizing discourse of the kind that had been increasingly welcomed by the *Review of English Studies* during the second half of the 1930s. Where it differs from such discourses (those associated with Bateson (pp. 81–2) and Wright (p. 88), for example) is in Leavis's insistence upon the 'exercise of the sense of value . . . controlled by an implicit concern for a total value-judgement', and based upon 'familiar' literary works, 'the nature and quality of which are immediately obvious'.[14] In the immediate post-war period, this discourse entered into the practical consciousness of many university teachers of English, eventually to such an extent that it significantly transformed the conditions of the discipline's reproduction. However, an understanding of how and why this happened requires a frame of reference much wider than one limited to the discipline of English.

The university in a democracy

Although Leavis's prescriptions were addressed most directly to the situation at Cambridge, their immediate impact was greatest within the newer university institutions. It is particularly instructive, therefore, to give some attention to those institutions which were either freshly conceived in the aftermath of the war, or which achieved university status at that time.

In 1946 a Committee at Stoke began planning a curriculum for what would become the University of Keele. A central figure for these deliberations was A. D. Lindsay, Master of Balliol College, Oxford. Lindsay proposed a general foundation course for all students consisting of the study of the 'Heritage of Western Civilization', 'Experimental Science', and 'Modern Democratic Institutions'.[15] Lindsay placed the central emphasis on 'culture', understood as 'the essential system of ideas governing the world and man, which belong to our time'. Thus, the primary function of the university was considered to be the teaching of 'the great cultural disciplines'.[16]

As James Mountford confirms, the stimulus of the war had generated a whole range of books about universities and their function, of which Leavis's was considered to be one of the most important examples. In the context of plans for Keele, Leavis's concern with bringing specialisms into communication was considered to offer a significant contribution to a sense of the function of universities in a 'democratic' society. For Lindsay, 'a democratic nation has to be a well-educated nation', and this necessitated combining the technical knowledge of the expert with the practical experience and understanding of the 'common life' of the ordinary public. Universities must therefore address directly the difficulties involved in reconciling expert knowledge with democracy.[17]

The great attraction of Leavis's discourse, then, is to be found in the possibility it seemed to offer of enacting such a 'reconciliation' by means of an education which was both culturally synoptic and evaluative. As will be seen, there were contemporary factors which favoured any programme that was sufficiently flexible to contribute to administering the 'common life', and thus able to contribute to a newly-important conception of 'vocational education'. For example, in the newly-founded *Universities Quarterly* in 1948, the Professor of the Philosophy of Education at University College London, Louis Arnaud Reid, emphasizes the contemporary need for 'a constant rethinking of the ways of education in the humanities'.[18] Without such rethinking, he argues, 'we shall lose our vision as a people, and, as a great people, surely perish, destroying more than ourselves in the process'.[19] For Reid, the current concern with the need to transform university education is related to the growing dependence of the universities on public funds and popular votes. Thus, it has now become necessary to justify and possibly improve arts education by showing how it may increase awareness of 'man' and 'the world'. A further factor is 'the present diminishing proportion (in relation to science and technology) of liberally educated persons'.[20] Indeed (if medicine and dentistry are excluded), the proportion of students studying for degrees in science and technology rose from 25.9 per cent to 32.6 per cent between 1938 and 1949, and rose even further to 40 per cent by the early 1960s. During the whole of this period, arts figures remained more or less static at 43–4 per cent.[21]

According to Reid, the 'diminished prestige' of arts education stems from its seeming remoteness and ornamentality, in that it produces no very evident tangible results.[22] To remedy this, he suggests that arts education must be shown to be 'vocational', which is to say that arts should be shown to provide education for living, acting, doing, knowing, thinking, and enjoying. Liberal education, conceived in this 'vocational' manner, would instil a 'habit of enlightened intuitive awareness and wisdom', thus breeding a sense of respect, flexibility of mind, and 'a sense of proportion'.[23] Of course, these were qualities very similar to the mental orientations claimed by Leavis to be fostered by his version of English. Indeed, this version of English was now beginning to be justified at some provincial universities on grounds of the kind proposed by Reid.

For example, Vivian de Sola Pinto (a regular contributor to the *Review* during the 1930s) had come to consider that in the post-war world liberally-educated persons, whether schoolmasters, civil servants, or business administrators should have the capacity to contribute to the revitalization of a 'soulless bureaucracy', and that the main object of English studies should therefore be 'the provision of a truly liberal education' for such 'non-specialists'.[24] Pinto had been Professor of English at Nottingham since 1938 and oversaw the university's transition to the autonomous degree-giving status which was achieved ten years later. Like Leavis, Pinto sees the pre-war pattern of English studies as blocking the development of a new conception of English as the centre of humanistic studies in a modern university. The earlier version of English at Nottingham as 'elegant dabbling in *belles-lettres*' stiffened by Anglo-Saxon and philology, now made way for a more Leavisian model: 'My conception of what a School of English should be was considerably clarified by my reading of Dr. Leavis' notable essay entitled "A Sketch for an English School" in his *Education and the University*.'[25] Furthermore, Pinto drew upon his experience as an external examiner for the Cambridge English Tripos in 1944–5, to develop a model of English for Nottingham which adapted the Cambridge course according to ideas gleaned from Leavis and another 'Scrutineer', L. C. Knights. This is very much in line with a wider emphasis on transmitting leadership qualities at Nottingham. As the historian of the university puts it: 'The war had amply proved the value to the community of men and women trained in the university as leaders, scientists and technicians.'[26]

It is interesting to compare the Nottingham view with that expressed by James Kinsley, the new Professor of English at Swansea, in 1954. At that time, Kinsley took issue with the 'common belief' that English could produce 'a unified human being capable of a ready and successful adjustment to the complex conditions of modern life, happy and with a sense of spiritual well-being'.[27] In keeping with a dominant impulse within inter-war English studies, he concludes that 'Literature constitutes a body of knowledge to be studied in and for itself without regard to any educational value it may have . . . [since] its being is its own justification.'[28] Unsurprisingly, given this position, he is insistent that Anglo-Saxon and philology be retained as essential features of English studies, even in the light of the growth of the discipline: 'Our first responsibility is to our subject, and, as that expands, we must not look for more ingenious methods of selection but for more time to do it justice.'[29]

In the changing circumstances of the post-war university such a position became increasingly untenable. In fact, even the backward-looking Kinsley was forced to amend his views on taking over as Professor at Nottingham in place of Pinto seven years later. He subsequently conceded that the views of English formed in the course of his own education at Edinburgh and Oxford had come to be modified in terms of 'Cambridge' notions. He admitted that, while English at Oxford and London had been 'admirable for training editors and literary historians', it was 'too inflexibly academic' to meet more general contemporary needs. This inter-war model of English studies was 'too "literary" to justify its central position in modern Arts studies', or to educate teachers and administrators for 'a changing society'.[30]

Thus, a number of professors of English and other influential educationalists were addressing themselves in the altered post-war environment to the issue of the disciplinary revisions required in order to produce 'enlightened' bureaucrats, administrators, and teachers. The influence of L. C. Knights upon Pinto has already been mentioned. Knights, who was Professor of English Literature at Sheffield from 1947 to 1952, shared this same concern, albeit developed along slightly more radical political lines. Writing in 1946, Knights, an editor of *Scrutiny* in the 1930s, is anxious that English should not avoid 'controversial questions' in the name of 'disinterested knowledge'.[31] The discipline should attempt to provide an education which produces men and women who are not afraid to ask awkward questions, particularly when it comes to matters relating to the 'quality of living', rather than being content to simply fit people into 'the machinery of society as it exists at present'.[32]

Knights is opposed to specialist training to a greater extent than the *Review* writers ever were before the war. For him the 'prevailing intellectual climate' cannot be relied upon to 'complement and complete specialist training'; nor can specialist training offer a 'discipline' suited to developing the sense of 'social responsibility' favoured by Knights.[33] The inter-war model of English studies, in its emphasis upon the past, has little to offer on those crucial 'cultural' questions of quality of living, 'human ends as well as means', or on the relations between culture and economic processes. In general Knights is concerned that English should enable students to address cultural issues which are of 'more than academic' importance, and have implications for a 'long-range programme for human betterment'.

It is essential for Knights that the discipline should attempt to relate the past, present, and future on an appropriately scholarly basis. Like Leavis before him and Raymond Williams at a later date, Knights concentrates attention on certain key words, especially 'the more important meanings of the word culture'.[34] However, he says, if English is to be constituted as a truly *cultural* subject, it must abandon the pre-war approach of 'covering the ground', and concentrate instead upon improving reading ability and training taste, which in turn requires a 'discipline'. Students of English should be trained, not only in the use of words 'for any and every purpose', but also in the 'discipline of strict literary criticism' since this is 'the only means we have of apprehending those embodied values with sureness and subtlety'. Literature may only be used as 'evidence' when it has first been assessed 'critically' as literature.[35]

In considering the attractions of this new discourse on culture, it is worth noting that, despite pressures to put a 'vocational' gloss on arts education, the mood of the post-war intelligentsia was in general moving to the right, away from a concern with social issues. It became conventionally acceptable to bemoan the difficulties involved in living a cultivated existence during a period of poverty and dislocation, often expressed in terms of the inevitability of failure, the absurdity of effort, and the necessity of resignation. Given this mood, there seemed to be much that was positive, radical, and energetic in the new English.[36] D. G. James, Winterstoke Professor of English at Bristol, urged the recognition that

> Education always has been, and always will be, a losing game. We shall get nowhere if we do not acknowledge this. Disillusion of this kind is rightminded, and, in addition, invigorating; it is the only possible antidote to despair, restlessness and languor which are always threatening.[37]

None the less, James could also acknowledge that 'There is no teacher of English in our universities more desirous and more able to make the study of English literature a living power than Dr. Leavis.'[38] And even a figure like John Butt (Professor of English at King's College, University of Durham (Newcastle)), associated with the *Review of English Studies* since the 1930s, and by 1951 its editor, favours Leavis's suggestion for studying a 'phase of civilization', such as the seventeenth century, rather than relying on 'factual information'. He also notes without disapproval the current popularity of presenting a 'critical judgement' as the text for discussion in English examinations, a novel post-war development.[39]

In general, then, the pressures for vocational relevance, together with attempts to transform English studies into an antidote to contemporary cultural debasement and conformity, helped to accredit the Leavisian critical approach. The same impulses also helped to instil within the profession the related need to build a 'free-floating' or 'disinterested' intelligentsia and a humanized bureaucracy. On this basis English became more closely attuned to producing individual citizens capable of full and critically evaluative responses, rather than the professional scholars and readers of the pre-war period. At least in intention, and at least at the peripheries of the profession, this represented a mode of accommodation within English studies to the demands of a 'democratic' order, and to the increased reliance of universities on public funds and popular votes. Of course the response to 'democratic' pressures was a highly modulated one. In practice the new discourse was addressed not to the population at large but to potential members of an elite of 'the educated'. The notion of 'culture' was an important feature within this process of modulation. The emphasis on 'culture' effectively distanced the study of English from wider social and political matters in the name of inculcating a general evaluative capacity or co-ordinated intelligence. 'Culture' provided a powerful countervailing force to those by now discredited attempts from the left during the 1930s to introduce 'class' as a category bearing on literature.[40] Liberty and individual freedom could now be defined in cultural rather than social or political terms as the free play of the human critical and evaluative impulse. The 'mature man' was thus placed at a distance equally from the 'blind' drive of the capitalist marketplace and a democratic process defined in quantitative or mechanical terms.

But, uniquely, the new English offered through education unmediated access to what was taken to be the central activity of all human judgement. Thus, in a situation where the contemporary social dynamic was seen as disordered and destructive, the new critical emphasis offered to intellectuals a mirror of their own estrangement and distance from everyday life, while holding up the ideal of a community of feeling and understanding based only upon literary criticism. The ideal was both 'modern' and at the same time conservative in its outlook. It offered a vision of a recoverable and unfragmented reality, personal integrity and wholeness, a free ontological movement within a world of values. However, 'culture' and 'art' were inherently undemocratic since they stood for processes of feeling, understanding, and evaluation that were considered to have become lost to majority cultures and literacies.

The new English also exhibited a considerable excess of ontological security when compared with the anxieties raised for pre-war English by the spectres of cynicism and ambiguity. English was, as it were, placed fully in the hands of the critic rather than the author, and the author would henceforth be admitted to the pantheon only on condition of a complete and 'first-hand' revaluation. Thus, the new version of English (often now explicitly distinguished from 'English Language and Literature') offered a sense of ontological security as well as a pedagogic programme, based particularly upon a conception of self-generating and autonomous value.

Challenges to the new English

Attractive as this new programme was as a response to the requirements of 'relevance', and the need to fight off incursions by scientific and technological education, it remained none the less vulnerable on a number of counts. The first area of instability was scholarship. For example, it has already been noted (p. 103) that D. G. James showed some sympathy for Leavis's work; but he also had some reservations regarding the new developments. He considered that English, seen as a form of study rather than the practice of cultivated reading, had still not freed itself from the criticism of lacking intellectual strenuousness.[41] In such a context, 'literary criticism' is 'viewed with a certain tolerant contempt', not only within the academic world at large but even within English schools themselves, especially by philologists. If the dangers of loss of prestige by the discipline are to be averted, James urged, not only must new measures such as joint schools and interdisciplinary studies be introduced, but the 'catastrophic decline' in the medieval side of English studies must be reversed.[42]

Helen Gardner, writing in 1959, is more concerned about the continued professionalization of English which has now rendered it a subject closed to all but experts, a condition for which the 'new' as much as the 'historical' critics must be blamed.[43] Gardner, a regular pre-war contributor to the *Review*, decries a loss of acceptance of English since the 1930s. She sees the discipline as 'once more under heavy fire' to an extent only comparable with the 1890s, and has no doubt as to the cause of this decline: the pernicious influence of the 'new critics'. Gardner deplores all attempts to train sensibility and taste or to inculcate critical standards and moral attitudes, and calls for a return to the pre-war emphasis on producing 'widely, intelligently and deeply-read scholars'.[44]

Similarly, in 1958, M. J. Collie accuses 'theoreticians' and 'self-styled humanists' of making 'a cult of their own profession' during the past fifteen years by fabricating 'a mysterious, nebulous value as the supreme end of literary study'.[45] He associates this post-war trend with the devaluation of a proper linguistic and historical discipline capable of searching out 'the meaningfulness of the text in its historical complexity'.[46] Collie then turns to what can be identified as the second area of instability within the new English: its claims to inculcate a sense of social responsibility. In opposition to the position espoused by Knights (see pp. 102–3), Collie sees the new English as freeing the individual *from* responsibility. He accuses the new critics of finding a value in art which falsely claims to give life order and meaning: 'The pursuit of literary value thus becomes the basis of a new morality. "Values" which were at first aesthetic have become didactic.'[47] The claims for English as an introduction to life are 'unfounded', the 'implicit educational creed in theory mistaken and in practice pernicious'. And, furthermore, in emphasizing literary value, the new English serves 'a power that is potentially cohesive in that it binds society into its proper heritage, and at the same time is wholly conservative'. It is not, argues Collie, the prerogative of English to save civilization. Instead it should address itself to instilling mental discipline, the capacity for argument, and the independent, sensitive, and rigorous sifting of evidence.[48]

But perhaps the most celebrated assault of all upon literary intellectuals as a group is made by C. P. Snow in his 1959 Rede Lectures.[49] On publication *The Two Cultures* was expected to sell between 1,000 and 1,500 copies, whereas in fact it sold over 100,000, resulting in an unprecedented public debate, and eventually extracting a reply from Leavis himself.[50] According to Snow, even the rise of modern science and technology had failed to displace the old pattern of training a small elite which characterizes English university education. He diagnosed the current situation as one in which the two cultures (literary intellectuals and scientists) had almost ceased to communicate with each other. Although it is the traditional culture which continues to manage the western world, Snow argued, only science can feed that world, create wealth, provide hope for the poor and the sick, and forge the essential links between intellect and practicality which make for a proper wisdom and awareness of moral and social issues.[51]

In the light of such attacks a number of attempts were made to resolve the problems posed for English, and liberal arts in general, by the need to demonstrate convincingly the social value of a humane education in a liberal democracy. One approach was to attempt to revise the idea of a liberal education so that it might provide guidance as to the proper application of science within society.[52] Within English itself there was already some awareness of the need to ensure that the discipline could touch the student of science: 'The student of the physical and social sciences is not a disembodied intelligence, and he too can gain much from that purifying of the emotions which is still one of the most valuable gifts of the literary artist to posterity.'[53] However, on the whole, English teachers at this time were content to defend their discipline on the grounds of its singular capacity to provide those 'human' values upon which the idea of a liberal education depended, and to present science and technology as merely an aspect of that mechanical world against which the 'battle of culture' needed to be pitched.[54]

Had it not been for one other factor, it seems likely that the combined pressures upon English both from inside and outside the discipline might well have caused it to accommodate itself more directly to the service of 'vocationalism', and 'social responsibility', and thus the needs of interdisciplinary and applied work. This factor was the entry of English into a period of even more buoyant growth, both of student and staff numbers, from the late 1950s. This acceleration of growth lessened the pressure on those areas of vulnerability discussed above and turned attention inwards towards the development and co-ordination of the discipline itself. This is evident from the attempts during the late 1950s and early 1960s to construct a generalist discourse which would encompass both the 'historical' and 'new critical' tendencies within English studies.

The most comprehensive efforts to provide new foundations for English studies at this time can be linked to the launching of the journals *Essays in Criticism* (founded in 1951, just prior to the demise of *Scrutiny*) and *Critical Quarterly* (founded 1958). *Essays in Criticism* was edited principally by F. W. Bateson, who announced in a preliminary circular the intention to tread midway between *Scrutiny* and *The Review of English Studies*.[55] The outcome has been assessed by Raymond Williams:

> In retrospect, what *Essays in Criticism* seems to have represented was the institutional absorption after the War of the so-called 'critical revolution' of the inter-war period, and the professionalisation of what had previously been a more or less oppositional movement within the academy.[56]

In many ways Bateson was the perfect person to oversee a transformation of this kind. As a respected Oxford academic, a socialist, and a regular contributor to the *Review* since the mid 1930s, he was in touch with the historical and modernist, governing and oppositional strands within the discipline. Furthermore, as will be seen, he had a personal commitment to the forging of an explicit relationship between English, education, culture, and the processes of liberal democracy.

In common with some other contributors to *Essays in Criticism* he had come around to the view that the object of English should be to develop in students a 'trained mind' rather than to produce 'literary critics' or even 'good readers'.[57] In his 1959 essay 'The English School in a Democracy' Bateson outlines the characteristics of the kind of trained mind he envisages, which seem to fit in with the mental attitudes and orientations most suited to the democratic process. For Bateson the operative principle of democracy is 'a balance or reconciliation of opposite or discordant qualities'.[58] In fact, this might be taken as a most apposite description of his own attempt at building a new consensus for English. Certainly the key objective is to find a means of aligning the discipline with the needs of contemporary society so as to justify claims for the centrality of English within university education. Furthermore, he was attempting to construct a discourse which was impervious to the kinds of attack then being launched from inside and outside the discipline. His solution to the problem of scholarship is to call for a closer alliance between literary criticism and the historical study of language, to be achieved through the kind of emphasis on literary language which he himself had favoured since the 1930s.[59] Subsequently he was to make it clear that this is not the language of 'linguistics' but a form of 'pre-verbal' communication. Access to this pre-verbal communication can be gained through those 'texts of the English classics' which constitute 'the supreme achievement of our race'.[60] It is important to note that it is on the basis of the self-evident cultural value of these texts that Bateson develops his sense of the wider relationship between culture and democracy.

He seeks to deflect any charges of over-specialization and methodological inadequacy by means of an appeal to the 'traditional values' of literature and the 'primacy of the text' for English studies.[61] The test of any methodology or specialized mode of study is the degree to which it illuminates rather than obscures the primary cultural values inherent in literature. These values are assumed to reside in the cultural continuum which Bateson sees as stretching from 1200 to the present.[62] It is, indeed, from these same constitutive values (inherent within the culture of this 'blessed isle') that 'the modern concept of democracy' has also arisen.[63] Thus, the university can make its most fruitful contribution to democracy through the teaching of an English which places the student in direct touch with the values embodied in the national literature. In the final analysis the specific method is merely a secondary affair, since any method must in the end efface itself:

> As the actual words and stylistic devices recede from the reader's consciousness their place is taken by an illusion of actual experience, one which the reader shares without actually being involved in it. An aesthetic distance . . .

separates the human situation which the reader appears to be contemplating from such a situation in real life.[64]

Bateson follows Richards, Bickersteth, and others in arguing that such experience is psychologically valuable provided that the reader approaches it as 'patient' rather than active interrogator.[65]

Perhaps most important of all, however, is Bateson's treatment of the issue of social responsibility. He is anxious that the student of English should gain a 'representative function'. Of course, if this could be established, English would be rendered relatively invulnerable to attacks of the kind mounted, for example, by Snow and Collie. Indeed, it is interesting that, in arguing that the critic should have 'the feel of the future in his bones', Bateson is repeating the exact formulation used by Snow to characterize the scientist.[66] The nature of this 'representative function' is best illustrated by considering the kind of student which Bateson wishes university English to produce. The object of a university should be to produce 'democratic individuals'. This necessitates transcending the simple 'imitative' pedagogy of the school, since democratic individuals require the kind of 'two-fold consciousness' which renders them 'capable of thinking their own thoughts' and 'feeling their own feelings'.[67] In order to achieve this, students require two qualities: 'self-identification' and 'verification'. The first of these is best achieved through 'criticism' and the second through 'scholarship', while the most effective means of combining them is through the study of English literature. What is required of the student is the capacity to identify with English: 'Unless an undergraduate can identify himself in some sense with the subject he is studying, he is either reading the wrong School, or has no business to be at university at all.'[68]

The reason given for the unique capacity of English to offer a truly democratic education is the peculiar nature of the poetic process:

The way a poet's mind works when he is being most a poet may be taken as the model of the process that operates as democracy in the political field and as education in the psychological field . . . A balance or reconciliation of opposite or discordant qualities is the operative principle (a) on the public plane in the twofold relationship between majorities and minorities in a democratic state, (b) on the private plane in the twofold self-consciousness that characterises the fully educated person.[69]

His conclusion is that English, if constituted according to these principles, is the university study not only best suited to produce the truly democratic individual, but the discipline which is 'destined in time to become the educational centre in English-speaking democracies'.[70]

It may be that a discourse like Bateson's which attempts to forge linkages between English studies and democratic processes was an unlikely candidate for acceptance within what has been described (by a university teacher active at this time) as the 'foppish, aristocratic atmosphere of the English university of the 1950s'.[71] The important point, though, is that the discourse touches many of the lines of force active within the discipline at that moment, and – despite subsequent transformations of the relationships between English, education, culture, and democracy – still active in the 1980s.

English as an integrated career structure

The impact upon English of university growth (and subsequently growth of non-university higher education) was considerable. On the one hand this expansion offered for the first time a substantial number of teaching posts which together formed a fully-integrated career structure, and on the other it considerably lessened the security of both the 'historical' and 'critical' paradigms for which Bateson had been at such pains to seek some form of mutual accommodation. In the course of the 1960s the boundaries of what counted as 'English' began to expand as more interdisciplinary and joint programmes of study were offered, especially at the new universities and later at the polytechnics.

By the mid 1960s the number of universities had doubled when compared to twenty years earlier, and the general undergraduate population had quadrupled. Rather than ministering to a small elite, these institutions had now established their function as the 'education of the upper intelligence groups of the nation', selected according to criteria which included being 'good' at English in school.[72] One much-remarked upon feature was the extent to which students now had in mind future career chances. The universities were seen less as 'finishing schools' and more as offering access to a career.[73] In response to this development some teachers of English began to justify the value of their discipline on the grounds that it offered 'an opportunity to discover both an individual identity and social role without premature commitment to a profession'.[74] While it remained possible to cling to a sense of the 'vital ambitions' of the discipline, 'human and institutional frailties' were seen as likely to inhibit the achievement of such ambitions. Continuing reliance might be placed upon the 'civilizing influence of literature'[75] but teachers were also aware that for many students a degree in English was simply a necessary preliminary to a career in business, commerce, the civil service, teaching, broadcasting, or journalism.[76]

Since the early part of the 1960s the sense that the universities needed to take their national role more seriously, as Reid had reminded them in 1948, had been somewhat enhanced by the appointment of the Robbins Committee. In fact the Government's 'minute of appointment' in 1961 set as the Committee's terms of reference to report on and review the pattern of full-time higher education in Britain 'in the light of national needs and resources'. Although the eventual Report addressed general principles rather than specific disciplinary practices, it did reiterate Reid's point that the 'financial dependence' of the universities made the direction of their development a matter of public interest.[77] While economic competitiveness was now presented as dependent upon the education of the nation's population, the drift of the Report was not purely towards an 'economistic' conclusion, 'culture' being another of its concerns (albeit a secondary one): 'Both in general cultural standards and in competitive intellectual power, vigorous action is needed to avert the danger of a serious relative decline in this country's standing.' However, within the university sector itself, the Robbins objective of assisting the maintenance of the country's 'standing' by transmitting 'a common culture and common citizenship'[78] was seen as problematic given the extent of the expansion taking place in the 1960s. For example, Albert

Sloman, Vice-Chancellor of the new University of Essex, while accepting the requirement of serving 'national need', considers that expansion has not been achieved without a 'drop in standards', despite Robbins's claim to the contrary.[79] He attributes this decline to the fact that students are now often entering university 'from homes with no tradition of culture or learning'. This, in fact, was a view shared by many teachers of English at the time. They would also have agreed with Sloman that, even before Robbins, it had become clear that universities were 'threatened by expanding numbers', and that radical measures were required to avert the dangers of such expansion to 'the traditional conception of a university'. John Butt, reviewing developments in English studies within the new universities in 1963, expresses the fear that adequate teaching and examining 'may be defeated by numbers'.[80] D. J. Palmer also argues that, more generally, post-war university expansion and the resulting rise in numbers taking English, has caused an influx of students unprepared for single subject study into the universities.[81] Indeed, as early as 1954, James Kinsley notes that 'it is no exaggeration to say that most of our students – Scots, English and Welsh alike – come to us hardly able to construe the English language, and unschooled in the patient, critical reading we require of them.' Furthermore, many of these students 'have not the degree of human sensibility needed for the complete assimilation of a poem. . . . As teachers . . . we cannot give this faculty to those who do not already possess it, as a natural endowment, in the degree which literary criticism demands.'[82]

Within the new universities one response to this perception of student 'inadequacy' was to engage in a certain amount of disciplinary 'cross-fertilization'; and to depend more upon the 'civilizing power' of a few 'great books' considered to have some contemporary 'relevance' than upon a 'professional' approach to English studies.[83] At Sussex, David Daiches took the view that the acquisition of knowledge must involve 'a world of cultural understanding that is *real*' for the student. Thus the study of English should allow some room for a 'dispassionate sociologico-cultural study of contemporary Britain'. But even more importantly perhaps, he considers that universities must actively transmit 'some idea of the stature of the English literary achievement' so that students may 'achieve the fullest possible awareness of the human relevance of works of literature'.[84] By the 1960s, English literature could no longer simply be relied upon to spontaneously generate within students a sense of its self-evident value.

Of course, the problem of 'relevance' had long been a familiar one to teachers of English within adult and working-class education. Richard Hoggart, for example, notes in 1951 that the adult tutor is necessarily forced to face challenges to the self-evident value of literature given the types of student involved. His own solution is one which was subsequently frequently used by teachers of English. Instead of viewing his task as that of a missionary to a 'primitive community', Hoggart seeks to encourage the development of what is 'already there'.[85] A different response to the issues of 'relevance', and perhaps the more common one within higher education from the 1960s, was to take the degree of 'adequacy' of literary awareness to be the measure of the individual student's 'intelligence' or 'maturity'. Allan Rodway and Mark Roberts, for example, argue that certain authors require 'too mature a taste' to be within the reach of 'any but the exceptional undergraduate'.[86] By the late 1960s various ways had been developed within English studies of dealing with the 'inadequacies' which resulted from the dissonances between student attitudes to literary study and teaching based on the elevated canon of great literary texts or 'classics'. Some teachers, in starting from 'what was there', even abandoned the attempt to expose students to 'the best that has been thought and said'. Instead they encouraged students to articulate their own experiences of frustration: 'the feelings which are articulated will point in the end – though the end may never be reached – towards a position of critical and perhaps revolutionary dissent from the established order of society'.[87]

Certainly, during this period it is common to find English teachers expressing a sense of the futility, or at least extreme difficulty, of attempting to influence in the direction of submission to great works of literature, students socialized into a culture of 'affluence'. As early as 1957, the apparent success of capitalism had led Hoggart to perceive a general progression 'towards a culturally "classless" society'.[88] At the same time, the 'whole way of life' towards which this change seemed to be directed was in conflict with the values of the 'literary tradition' of which most English teachers still considered themselves the guardians. This conflict drew a wide range of responses from within English from the late 1950s into the 1970s. Some took the view that it was essential that English be made less 'remote from the living interests of the average adolescent'.[89] A few even attempted to move literary education in the direction of political 'confrontation'.[90]

Hoggart himself seeks a more interdisciplinary and sociological resolution. At first he considers that the conflict between literary values and contemporary culture can be resolved in a typically modernist manner, in that literature can be the means of subverting 'conventional' views of life.[91] Later he attempts to move beyond 'purely literary values'[92] towards more 'organic' studies which 'begin in close cultural reading [of literary texts] and can lead out, in conjunction with other disciplines, into better cultural analysis'.[93] None the less, Hoggart emphasizes the primary need to 'submit' to works of art, even when they are being used as social documents.[94] Of course, the sense of the danger to English studies from viewing literary texts as social, historical, or cultural 'documents' reached back at least as far as Newbolt, and every subsequent suggestion that texts be used in such a way rekindled related anxieties.[95] But the issue was now raised in its sharpest ever form by the wider perception of a 'crisis in the humanities' due to the incapacity of university structures to attune themselves to contemporary cultural and economic needs.[96] The renewed interest in using literary texts as a means of inculcating the kind of critical competence which could comprehend rather than simply dismiss contemporary culture in all its complex manifestations, was one kind of response to this crisis.

Crisis in the humanities

The sure sense of the unchallengable humanistic basis for English studies, upon which for example Bateson's justification of the value of the English school in a democracy rested, became increasingly difficult to sustain from the 1960s. The end of the 1950s had seen the eclipse of 'the last epoch of the dominance of literary criticism in English culture' and the emergence of cultural styles appropriate to consumer capitalism (qualitatively new kinds of magazine, advertisements, television programmes, and political campaigning, for example).[97] By 1969, Leavis is to be found expressing his 'sense of the urgent gravity' of the contemporary cultural situation, 'a frightening face of the gravity being the blankness – the inability or refusal to perceive – that characterises our civilization'.[98]

The consequences for English studies of the reassessment of liberal humanism in the light of the experience of war and the subsequent emergence of the 'affluent society', and popular and youth cultures, is perhaps best examined through George Steiner's 'after Auschwitz' thesis. Reflecting on the extermination of 70 million human beings in recent times, Steiner argues that

> what man has wrought on man . . . has affected the writer's primary material – the sum and potential of human behaviour – and it presses on the brain with a new darkness . . . We know that some of the men who devised and administered Auschwitz had been trained to read Shakespeare and Goethe, and continued to do so.

For Steiner, this revelation puts into question the 'primary concept of a literary, humanistic culture'.[99]

Introducing the collection of essays, *Crisis in the Humanities*, in which Steiner's essay appeared in 1964, J. H. Plumb calls for 'less reverence for tradition and more humility towards the education systems of those two great countries – America and Russia – which have tried to adjust their teaching to the urban, industrial world of the twentieth century'.[100] Graham Hough develops this argument as applied to English studies by claiming that the Christian-humanist ideal is now worn and battered, with a resulting confusion within literary education. The traditional 'upper-bourgeois literary education' which was addressed to the scholar–gentleman–Christian, has, Hough declares, become irrelevant to the contemporary world. Despite all claims to the contrary, English, rather than being at the core of the humanities, has become 'merely one subject among others'.[101] Even the attempted revisions of the discipline associated with the *Scrutiny* programme have failed due to its lack of positive practical goals: 'False ideals are not destroyed merely by seeing through their linguistic dress, but by opposing them with stronger and better ones.' The new critics' belief that 'a new organon, a whole new range of intellectual apparatus, had come into being' has proved to be 'an illusion'. Indeed, criticism's aspiration to deal with 'the whole conditions of intellectual health in a society' is now shown to be misconceived.[102] Only the 'ideal' of the professional scholar is left, which is remote both from the 'interests of unprofessional readers' and from all students of literature except the 'brightest'.[103] The current situation is one of chronic 'academic paralysis'. Not only is most pre-modern literature now culturally remote, but England is no longer the centre of contemporary literary creation in the English language.[104] In sum, it is no longer possible for English studies to rely upon traditional literary values, given current awareness of a history dominated by privation, sectarianism, and nationalism.[105] The future of English studies depends for its success upon establishing a 'coherent body of knowledge' for the discipline, and attempting to shape imaginatively the new 'teen-age sub-cultural ideal' now being formed.

This kind of critique of the traditional gentlemanly and humanistic, and even new-critical, basis of English became ever more common in the course of the 1960s and later. For example, the *Times Literary Supplement* had always been ready (from the point of view of the literary culture of the 'man of letters') to criticize academic English studies for its increasing distance from the lay literary world. In a 1968 editorial it notes the 'present muddled, unsatisfactory situation' within English, and recommends that the discipline finally abandon its claim to provide 'morally nutritive properties' and simply accept that literature is worth studying for 'its own sake'.[106]

Despite the occasional call for a militant renewal of the Leavisian enterprise, by 1970 every one of its fundamental ideological props had been subjected to considerable strain. Not all the attacks were, however, launched from the same platform. By the late 1960s, and even more forcefully from the middle 1970s, an alternative 'stance for combat' had been successfully developed.

The rise of the new right

In reconsidering *Education and the University* in 1968, W. W. Robson accepts that liberal education now requires 'apology', given the widespread loss of faith in its relevance, and the fact that the measure of agreement about essential values is now so much less than it was. His solution is the pragmatic one, common at the time, which involves establishing as large and vague a syllabus as possible and leaving a great deal of choice to students. However, there is another aspect of his position which has more in common with the revisionary as opposed to liberalizing tendency within the discipline. This is to be found in Robson's assertion that the concept of 'democracy' is inapplicable to the Arts, since compositional capacity is 'uncommon' and critical appreciation even less so.[107]

C. B. Cox and A. E. Dyson also writing in 1968, recall that *Critical Quarterly* had been founded in 1958 with the intention of opposing that kind of cultural 'pessimism' associated with the sense of a 'breakdown of classic humanism' of Steiner's 'after Auschwitz' thesis.[108] While Cox and Dyson share in the opposition to *Scrutiny*'s 'negative anti-contemporary' attitudes, the grounds on which they do so are very different from those put forward by Hough, Falck, and other critics of Leavisism. For these editors of *Critical Quarterly*, and from 1969 of the influential *Black Papers*, 'Great literature helps to keep alive our most subtle and delicate feelings, our capacity for wonder, and our faith in human individuality. The artist contributes to the vitality of language, to the preservation of the Word in the desert.'[109] There remains here a certain sense of uneasiness in the face of the 'desert' of contemporary culture which reaches back to Dyson's account of the 'younger' universities published in *Critical Quarterly* almost a decade earlier. Writing in 1959 of the teaching of English in these universities, Dyson expresses a certain pessimism in the light of the powerlessness of 'men of liberal principles' to perform their proper function as guardians of 'civilized values'.[110] If the university is to act as the 'cultural centre for the whole community', with literature as the 'central civilizing force', it needs to be capable of discrediting those students who 'are actually too lazy or incompetent to do an honest day's work'. In actively opposing laziness and incompetence, the teaching of English should 'heighten respect for individual freedom', and develop loyalty towards 'the finest achievements and possibilities of the race'.[111]

Thus, even in 1959, the antidote to pessimism as much as to incompetence involves the imposition of 'physical and mental discipline' capable of countering what another *Critical Quarterly* contributor calls the 'debilitating hedonism of a "good-time" civilization'.[112] During the 1960s this tendency within English studies developed a consistent right-wing assault on all forms of cultural and educational egalitarianism. The basis of their programme is clearly outlined in an inaugural lecture given by G. H. Bantock at Leicester in 1965. Given the influence over the culture and literacy of the majority of the population of an 'unpropitious environment' and 'alternative cultural media', Bantock claims that attempts through education to impose a 'book culture' on this majority merely inflict upon them an unacceptable 'strain'.[113] In any case, 'the education we provide' is said to produce 'on a considerable section of the population few or no results'. According to Bantock, because of the nature of the community from which 'this section' springs, they are 'unable to face up to the psychological demands' of 'literate culture'. He proceeds to draw upon Bernstein's work in supporting the view that equality 'is being used to make more difficult any possibility of evolving a system of education adjusted to the varying levels of cultural and mental capacity in our community'. Egalitarians are therefore pronounced guilty of 'sentimentality' for failing to 'accept the complexity of human existence as it actually faces us'.[114]

It requires only a small further step to argue for the exclusion from English of 'those unfitted to benefit' from studying literature. Indeed, in 1968, T. R. Henn is to be found recommending that at Cambridge the number of students taking English should be cut by 40 per cent on the grounds that many students tend simply to 'drift' into the discipline. For Henn, 'the delicacy and complexity of the response of the individual, and the crucial importance of the values transmitted, makes any system of mass-instruction pernicious'.[115]

These themes were summarized and developed by a large group of contributors writing for the *Black Papers* between the late 1960s and mid 1970s, which had a considerable impact on educational debates, and indeed on public policy.[116] The contributors regularly asserted that a university was not a democracy, and that academic study should be reserved for an elite by concentrating attention and opportunity only upon students endowed with 'unusual gifts'. By the late 1970s this avowedly elitist tendency had provided an attractive and powerful rallying-point for those in English studies who saw it as their function to 'uphold the finest academic and cultural values'. Teachers of this persuasion wished to accept for admission to higher education, and to English studies, only those students possessing a sufficiently high level of 'qualitative literacy'[117] and sufficiently hard-working and disciplined as well as competitively-motivated to 'benefit' from university education. From this perspective, the capacity to appreciate literary texts had become the measure of the achievement of 'qualitative' as opposed to 'functional' literacy. As Michael Paffard puts it in 1978: 'Not all men [are] equally qualified by learning or experience to make value judgements about literature or to be called literary critics.'[118] While 'functional literacy' guarantees the capacity to engage in normal communication within one's given 'culture or group', it does not guarantee the capacity to distinguish between good and bad in literature. For Paffard to ask whether a piece of writing is 'literature' is to ask whether it is 'good'. Furthermore, the perception of such goodness requires a posture of submission on the part of the student of English: 'His discipline, like that of all disciplines, will lie in a willing submission to a master or masterpiece.' In this manner literature fulfils the need for 'assurances of value from guides we respect'.[119]

By the 1970s, all of the familiar themes associated with the post-war new-critical programme had been appropriated by the new right and the humanistic sense that English departments might play a central and autonomous role in the transformation of the general 'quality of life' in society had all but collapsed. Leavis himself is by now reduced to an expression of gratitude for the letters page of *The Times* in 'the world of triumphant modernity, the world of power-centres from which the quantity-addicted machinery of civilization is controlled, directed and exploited' and in which 'literature in the old sense has ceased to matter'.[120] Henceforth the conception of English as a central force for sustaining the national cultural 'heritage' would become largely the property of the right.

The pluralist consensus

Apart from the emergence of the new right, there were other factors which contributed to a loss of the sense of cultural centrality within the discipline of English studies during the 1970s. The establishment within English of a fully integrated career structure encouraged more pragmatic attitudes towards the discipline. In 1972 the *Times Literary Supplement* carried, over a number of issues, a survey into the state of English in various universities.[121] One notable feature to emerge from these reports is the loss of faith, at least among younger academics, in what the *TLS* Special Correspondent calls the old 'mystical' attitude, an insistence on the special power of English to exert a civilizing influence. The teaching of English was now often viewed simply as a desirable job and staff were often motivated more by their desire to pursue a comfortable career than by any wider sense of social function.[122] Keith Brown and Christophe Campos had already argued in 1971 that

> An impressive university department might be staffed with the established academics who have lately confessed, in print, to basic doubts about the validity and purpose of English literary studies; and it is hard today to think of any branch of formal literary study that does not reflect something of the same malaise.[123]

But in the 1970s students were flooding into English studies in previously unparalleled numbers across the range of relatively diverse institutions of higher education including the ancient and newer 'civic or provincial' universities, the post-war 'plateglass' universities, and the polytechnics. It would be true to describe the discipline as having achieved an astounding success if such success is measured in terms of the establishment of English literature as the central arts subject at A level, and thus at the basis of the constant demand for undergraduate places. Furthermore, at the levels of teaching and research, the discipline was now able to offer wide and attractive career opportunities to its most successful graduates. It is perhaps not surprising that, in such circumstances, the older defensive logics of the discipline, and especially the *petit-bourgeois* critical consciousness of the *Scrutiny* tendency, could no longer offer a generally acceptable disciplinary ideology. However, if many academics now felt that overt humanism had been discredited, there was little evidence of any major displacement of the 'classics of English literature' from the centre of disciplinary practice. 'English', especially in the newer institutions, was becoming a process of overseeing, encouraging, and measuring the capacity to write about these classic texts in an interesting, imaginative, and knowledgeable manner. It was now generally agreed (despite claims to the same effect reaching back to the 1930s and beyond) that the map of literary history was as complete as it was ever likely to become.[124] Thus the production of original approaches to, or interpretations of, the major texts had become the focus for almost all writing by English academics. Indeed, the discipline itself was often characterized as 'criticism', and its history seen as a succession of critical paradigms or approaches.[125]

Graham Hough is surely only partially accurate when he claims that

> The great attraction of Schools of English in the universities is no longer primarily literature. It is that they are so flexible, so accommodating, especially in some of the newer forms. An able and wayward mind can make almost what it will of them.[126]

The increase in flexibility may be conceded, although it should be added that it commonly only extended to the classic texts, most notably the works of Shakespeare, whose assumed centrality continued to be justified in terms both of their uniquely potent literary rhetoric,[127] and their cultural and imaginative force within 'the pool of our common experience'.[128] As will be seen, any attempt to question such assumptions was likely to raise the question, sometimes in quite an explosive form, as to whether the study could be authorized as 'English' at all.

Thus, despite the development since the 1970s of a whole plethora of 'critical' and 'theoretical' approaches to literature, English studies remained (and remains still) radically inconceivable without those texts which authorize it as an area of

English and *literary* study. Certainly, it may be admitted that as a consequence of challenges to humanism, the overt force of the national concept within English studies has been diminished (but far from extinguished), and the space for a new and valuable concern with methodology has been opened up. What has not been substantially deflected, however, is the practical assumption (in teaching, if not in theory) of an unchanging literary essence which is taken to inhere within some or other selection of English texts, irrespective of any introduction of parallel, contextual, or complementary studies.[129]

A consistent theme within English studies since the 1970s has been the call for a 'methodology' capable of describing and analysing the 'nature of the knowledge specific to English as a discourse',[130] or at least offer a 'fully articulated and logically coherent appraisal which could count as indubitable knowledge about a given literary work'.[131] Hilda Schiff points out that such a methodology would considerably stabilize the teaching of English in that students could then be expected to 'master' an identifiable body of knowledge. Such calls have not gone unheeded, and they have even encouraged, to however limited an extent, the kind of analysis of the 'modes of operation' whereby English teachers 'pursue their own work', for which Schiff also calls.[132]

But more characteristically the response has been a massive importation into academic English studies of theories and methods otherwise associated with structuralism, linguistics, semiotics, sociology, marxism, and post-structuralism. However, as Patrick Parrinder has pointed out, most of these approaches – in their concern with methodology rather than with the aims and purposes of English studies – have led to changes in manners of interpretation rather than in the choice of texts: they do not usually lead to any significant reconsideration of the worth of pursuing the interpretation of texts as such.[133] As Parrinder also indicates, the question remains as to whether the 'aims of English' can be formulated other than in terms of humanism, a question which will be considered in the Conclusion.

Perhaps one reason for the paucity of attempts to offer a direct critique of the 'aims of English', is the tendency within the discipline to avoid overt and detailed manifestos or statements of aims and objects upon which such critiques might be based. Only at moments when pressure has been exerted by groups seeking some radical reorientation of the discipline, or when reorientation has been fiercely resisted, have manifestos of any substance appeared: Churton Collins's campaign against Oxford in the 1890s, the Newbolt Report which developed out of the initiatives of the English Association, the *Scrutiny* movement, and most recently, the new right. My argument here is that the recent emphasis on flexibility has generated pluralist consensus within English which represents a further refusal to articulate an underlying basis and a clear set of aims and principles for the discipline; and that this refusal, when understood in relation to the appropriation by the new right of the residues of the humanist programme, forms a significant characteristic of the continuing crisis in English studies.

It has already been indicated that the tendency towards greater 'flexibility' within newer forms of English was noted by Graham Hough as early as 1970. Garry Watson, in attacking the new pluralism from a Leavisian perspective, offers two exemplary passages by contemporary academic critics which may serve as illustrations of this trend:

> many of the critics I most admire have taken all the latitude in the world, and have earned the right to such freedom by the extraordinary power of their perceptions, many of them being achieved by critical reverie.[134]

> the only works we value enough to call classic are those which, as they demonstrate by surviving, are complex and indeterminate enough to allow us our necessary pluralities.[135]

Examples of this kind could readily be multiplied, but it does not follow that the different methods espoused are really all that different in their fundamental orientations.[136] Even more to the point is the actual rarity of defences of the pluralist position. It is clear from the general discussion above, that earlier positions were forged out of identifiable institutional and cultural campaigns and struggles, and indeed the fundamental orientations of pluralism were only rendered explicit in a comparable situation of crisis at the end of the 1970s, by which time the attractions of the new pluralism had long been established.

In the early part of the decade the term 'pluralism' regularly cropped up at newer institutions such as the University of East Anglia, and, as was noted by a *TLS* correspondent, this term was 'invariably meant to signal virtue'.[137] In fact, 'pluralism' was as much a term for describing institutional arrangements as for emphasizing varieties of approach or methodology. As is still the case, students at some universities in the early 1970s could build their own pattern of course units in ways which tended to displace the historical chronology of literature associated with 'English Language and Literature'. Indeed, in 1979 Pat Rogers of the University of Bristol relates the passing of the earlier crisis in English studies to the rise of the new pluralism: 'There is, thank goodness, no great crisis of confidence in English Studies . . . All those anxious and fretful tracts of a decade or so ago – on the frontiers, or the task, or the business, or the identity of criticism – have a slightly comic air today.'[138] The discipline can now offer 'competing ideologies' and 'alternative brands to sample'. There is no longer any need to ask whether 'the whole discipline of criticism' has a future. It is interesting to note, though, that Rogers feels able to identify the factors which anchor this plurality of approaches to a fundamentally literary essence. For Rogers, literature is 'logically prior' to literary study. Thus, whatever approach is to be taken, there is a prior requirement of 'respect for the text' as a human utterance, expressive gesture, and aesthetic object.[139] The goal of the study of English is to enrich 'our appreciation of particular books' rather than to construct 'a psychology of literary response' or develop 'a sociology of literary consumption'. It is clear that the books in question are those of 'considerable writers', and that to 'study literature' means to concentrate on the texts which, by virtue of 'the special skill of a gifted minority', enshrine 'the most intense experience of the race'. Continuing upon the familiar submissive theme, Rogers asserts that while the apprehension of 'great art in its fullness is a goal none of us can hope fully to attain', it remains 'a worthy objective just the same'.[140]

It is clear then, that the rise of pluralism, both interpretative and methodological, has not necessarily displaced the central ideological themes of the past. Indeed, Rogers appears to allow this apparently 'genial ecumenicalism'[141] to be infused with the priorities of the new right. The ideological boundaries of the whole pluralist enterprise will come into even sharper focus when we consider the 'Cambridge Crisis' below.

The survival of practical humanism

Before considering the 'Cambridge Crisis', it is important to look at an aspect of English studies which is often ignored. It may be that the central significance of modern manifestations of the humanist impulse is to be found at the practical rather than the methodological or theoretical level. Tony Davies, for example, has said that 'the real effectivity of "literature" as a practice' is to be found in the humdrum activity of English teaching. However, he continues, it would be wrong simply to seek an account of actual practices within 'critical' work: instead, it is necessary to attend to the 'disjointed and episodic philosophy' which is activated in the course of ordinary teaching.[142]

Perhaps this is of particular importance when considering the more informal pedagogies which have played a major part in teaching activity since the late 1960s. Barbara Hardy already takes the view in 1975 that some amendment to practical modes of teaching is needed given that many students find no affinity with the Leavisian critical stance, nor 'share the faith in Englishness and European civilization'. Thus, they are now likely to 'come up and challenge the very life-affirmation for its smugness, complacency, and lack of eloquence'.[143] Hardy provides a good example of a wider kind of practical response to a perceived shift of 'taste', and the need to develop forms of English teaching of sufficient flexibility to be extended beyond the traditional narrow student elite. The response certainly illustrates the transition to a less 'intransitive' pedagogy and more 'interpersonal style': 'Questions are coming up from the students. It is getting harder to stay behind the rostrum and teach without learning.'[144]

Teachers like Hardy were well aware of the need for adaptations of the kind which Davies associates with a wider shift from 'authoritative monologue' to 'open-ended conversation':[145]

Let us accept the shifting of taste, and let us show our faith in the Great Tradition by teaching as much as possible of the literature we admire, without worrying too much about canons and with attention to variety rather than moral unity. Let us admit that good taste and proper judgement have to be worked out slowly and painfully and personally, and that it is each man for himself.[146]

Tony Davies positions the move towards informal modes of interaction within larger institutional transformations. The correlation between this kind of development within English and changes within the 'welfare' services is made clear by John Broadbent in his description of the influences bearing upon his teaching practice at the University of East Anglia.[147] Here again there is an attempt at finding more flexible modes of negotiation between the tradition of 'literary culture' and contemporary student experience: 'My motives also included a more protestant kind of regression, to re-establish links between literary culture – cherished and transmitted by an elite of abstract expertise – and experience.' For this reason he 'began to study group behaviour', and came to the conclusion that 'role-play is in itself interdisciplinary, interactive. I learned about it from another culture, from social workers and counsellors.' According to Broadbent, it is no longer desirable to 'ignore the resources of experience that students bring to higher education . . . it is by activating those resources *in the academic arena* that we might respond creatively to protest.'[148]

Similarly, Hardy found herself confronted by 'some unanticipated possibilities of rejecting Lit. Crit.'. It seemed now that perhaps 'one could go on talking about human needs and problems, teaching and learning about imagination, even if all the books were burnt'.[149] The books have not been burnt, but none the less the talking continues, and the force of its 'humanism' derives as much from the everyday exchanges (tutorial and seminar) as from formal critical, theoretical, or methodological notions. Tony Davies attests to the continuing force even in the 1980s of the 'fluid and contradictory debris of discursive fragments' which surrounds such limp, but none the less coercive, questions as 'Well, what do you think of this then?'[150] It seems that what continues largely to hold these fragments together are those practically-embedded assumptions into which

Barbara Hardy, in her strict attention to the humdrum inter-
actions rather than the more formal discursive superstructure,
offers a degree of insight unusual for writings on English in
higher education. Certainly Hardy's account gives weight to
Davies's claim:

> the relative informality and openness of literature teaching,
> its disinclination to impose judgements or dictate pre-given
> conclusions, itself constitutes a determinate discursive
> regime, constrained by its own rules, limits and positionali-
> ties: a regime that can be characterised as 'liberal' in so far as
> it imposes itself not by insisting on the positional authority of
> the teacher, nor by compelling assent to a given and explicit
> curriculum of knowledge, but by inviting a voluntary reco-
> gnition of the existence, purpose and value of a 'subject':
> Literature itself.[151]

However, it is surely necessary to agree also with Davies's
further observation that, to recognize the underlying force of
such relatively informal and open modes of teaching is not
necessarily to argue for a return to earlier more authoritative
and intransitive modes.

It is worth observing, furthermore, that even a committed
liberal humanist teacher like Barbara Hardy found that opportunities to teach 'against the environment' were rare;[152]
perhaps particularly so in that her own college (Birkbeck)
worked within the examination-dominated regime of the
University of London.[153] Even minor amendments of the kind
introduced under Quirk and Kermode at University College in
the period when Hardy was writing this account generated
misgivings in the other London colleges. Far from contemplating the burning of books, any amendments which inhibited
coverage of 'the whole corpus of English literature' were considered dangerously radical.[154] In fact, on the whole, London –
like Oxford – made fewer concessions to the liberal practices of
collaborative seminar discussion than did the newer
institutions.

The Cambridge Crisis

It was Harold F. Brooks, a colleague of Hardy's at Birkbeck
College, who contributed to the debate on English studies at

Cambridge carried by the press and other media early in 1981, by complaining that 'much of the resort to 'isms and 'ologies' amounts to 'duncery', and is thus 'a menace to the common-wealth of letters, and so to civilization'. For the now-retired Brooks, it remains

> The paramount duty of a university teacher of literature . . . to show his students the ways by which great art creates its effects, leading them to a finer appreciation and fuller re-sponse, and to help them appreciate more fully the authors' insights, so often deeper than our own [sic], contribute towards our understanding of ourselves, our community, and life itself.[155]

Brooks, it would seem, was in no position to comprehend the impact made by the new pluralism at Cambridge. While Cambridge had offered little concession to seminar teaching, it had allowed space for the introduction of a plurality of critical approaches and methodologies. Even at Cambridge this had not been plain sailing, as the remarks attributed to Christopher Ricks make clear:

> Obviously, no one objects to the presence of structuralists and theorists of film and linguistics in the English faculty. But there is a question of proportion. It is our job to teach and uphold the canon of English literature.[156]

The occasion for these pronouncements was provided by the 'Cambridge Crisis': an occasion which offers an instructive case-study of the practical and institutional boundaries of the spirit of 'genial ecumenicalism' supposedly characteristic of the new pluralism.

By the early 1980s, it had become possible to study modern linguistics, structuralism, semiotics, marxist theory, post-structuralism, the sociology of literature, various brands of specifically literary theory, and cultural studies in some or other relation to English at a number of polytechnics and universities.[157] In May 1981 Colin MacCabe was appointed at the age of 31 as Britain's youngest Professor of English to oversee the progress of this kind of development (particularly in the direction of film and television studies) at the University of Strathclyde. Like a number of other English departments and Schools of Humanities within the newer universities and the polytechnics, Strathclyde had already developed some work in the fields of modern literature and linguistics, and wished to expand research and teaching within other areas of contemporary cultural study.[158] MacCabe was appointed to the professorship because he was seen at Strathclyde as 'one of the ablest men of his generation', having 'an outstanding record in teaching and research'.[159] This appointment brought to an end five months of unprecedented coverage in the media of the condition of English studies. During its life, the 'MacCabe affair' called forth such novelties as the Sunday 'Heavies' wrestling with Levi-Strauss, a whole range of bluffers' guides to 'structuralism' in the broadcast and print media, and even the ultimate accolade of a *Punch* cartoon about the capture of 'the Cambridge structuralist'.[160]

Two features of the 'Cambridge Crisis' should be noted here. First is the fact that the same person should be so highly regarded by one English department while being accused of engaging in 'discredited intellectual enquiry' in another;[161] second is the fact that the failure to offer a tenured post to an English teacher at Cambridge should provide the occasion for such unparalleled radio, television, and newspaper coverage of English studies. A review of this coverage supports the conclusion that the refusal of tenure to MacCabe was related to a sense among Cambridge traditionalists that the time had come to mount a strong resistance to further incursions by the tendency MacCabe was thought to support. The objection was not to his mode of teaching, but to his association with intellectual forces which were seen as foreign to the task of 'upholding the canon of English literature'. The resistance was not new, although in this case its impact was dramatic.

In fact, as the *THES* noted at the time, the dispute leading to this crisis had been simmering in relative privacy for some time.[162] The genealogy of these developments is significant for understanding recent movements within English studies. While in 1960 Cambridge English had been still in the process of accommodating traditional canonical scholarship to the revisions of the new criticism, by the end of that decade this process had been displaced in the name of a pluralism of approaches.[163] By then Leavis had retired and, although L. C. Knights had been appointed Regius Professor, the ideal of

practical criticism seemed no longer sufficiently strong to provide an adequate focus for 'intellectual and imaginative' work.
Students had begun to be exposed to a range of different approaches such as Steiner on comparative literature and linguistics, Raymond Williams on cultural studies, John Holloway
on structural analysis, and an assortment of others ranging
from traditional historical criticism to contemporary continen-
tal theory. The instability of such pluralism was revealed in the
'brawl' which accompanied attempts to amend the paper entitled 'The history and theory of literary criticism' in 1972.[164]
A working party comprised of Williams, Holloway, and Hough
proposed the introduction of a new paper on 'Literary theory:
selected topics' which would cover symbol and myth, the
language of literature, and literature and marxism. George
Watson, responding to this proposal, asserted that such topics
were inappropriate for a course leading to a degree called
'English', and in any case dismissed both marxism and structuralism as outmoded 'intellectual dinosaurs': 'No doubt a
university is the place to study discredited intellectual systems;
but we risk derision if we propose them to the exclusion of
others.'[165] That no final accommodation between these diverse
conceptions of the boundaries of English was achieved is clear
from the re-emergence of precisely the same arguments, but
now within a much wider public domain, in 1981. Watson's
remarks in a BBC Radio 4 interview reiterated his views of
almost a decade earlier.[166] The position remained substantially
the same as that described by Raymond Williams at the time of
the earlier confrontation: 'The consensus on which the English
faculty did its best work ended about the time of Leavis's
retirement and a new consensus has yet to be worked out.'[167]

However, by 1981, in the context of wider cultural and social
movements to the right, the proponents of the older conception
of English felt strong enough to launch a direct attack on the
new pluralism, or, at the very least, to insist that this pluralism
be grounded firmly in the study of the 'classics of English
literature'. There were particular reasons why this should have
happened at Cambridge. At the newer universities and
polytechnics the process of institutional growth had led to a
variety of adjustments both in modes of teaching (most notably
through the introduction of the seminar) and curriculum (with

a more modern and selective emphasis, and the use of the period study). The same had not been true at Cambridge. Even by the 1980s, seminar teaching had found little hold there despite a decreasing proportion of staff to students. Indeed both Oxford and Cambridge had become, relatively speaking, seriously understaffed over the previous decade despite the fact that at each university about 900 students were now reading English, three times as many as in 1965.[168]

In effect, the uneasy pluralist consensus had been pushed into crisis through pressures of growth, and in the process had revealed the political basis of the underlying conflict. However, rather than leading to a debate on the nature and aims and purpose of English studies, the Cambridge Crisis generated, on the one hand, a defence of pluralism, and, on the other, a retrenchment in the name of the unique value of the English classics. By comparison with the situation in 1972, these disputes now carried a much stronger political and cultural resonance outside the university: while both factions at Cambridge resolutely denied that the crisis was a political one, no such refusal was seriously accepted by the media. At the same time, while it was now impossible to recover any significant sense of the centrality of English within the process of political democracy, the Cambridge Crisis allowed the wider debates about the 'democratic' process to come into play within English studies. The situation was now very different from that in the 1950s when defences of the value of the English literary canon could be mounted on the basis of the educational centrality of English studies, or of its psychological force, or even of its humanism.[169] The necessity for submission to greatness had now come to be placed in stark opposition to a scholarly pluralism. The politics of English studies were revealed in a confrontation between a fundamentally right-wing educational philosophy and a countervailing defence of the need for a plurality of emphasis. The defence of pluralism, however, was aligned to professional scholarship rather than a clearly formulated politics of education. Stephen Heath argued for MacCabe's appointment on the grounds of the need to sustain the Cambridge English faculty as the 'greatest in the world'.[170]

Conclusion:
Fiction, culture, and society

We must now attempt to assess the extent to which the foregoing history can contribute to an understanding of the contemporary condition of English studies, and how it can identify possible and desirable changes. The early initiatives culminating in the publication of the *Newbolt Report* were an attempt to invent a new identity for English as a centre for national cultural mobilization and renewal. Despite occasional protestations to the contrary, this moment has well and truly passed. Indeed, as I have shown, with the inter-war failure of the early initiatives, the discipline came largely to be constituted and ordered according to rigorous and exclusive professional norms. In effect, the project of a national 'popular' mission was replaced by the goal of offering to a select few some kind of credible experience of harmonious release from the harsh realities of capitalist exchange. Since that moment the masculine professional identity upon which the 'Englishness' of English has been grounded has served to provide a stable relation between discourses on language, literature, humanity, nationality, and education. While subsequently there have been a number of attempts to breach this professional bulwark and propagate a new sense of social function for English, it now seems more certain than ever that English cannot be established as a national cultural mobilizing centre.[1] Certainly, the varied pressures of adapting to post-war democracy did generate the sense of an urgent need to reinvest the discipline with symbolic potency. However, given that the social function of high culture has subsequently been attenuated to a conservational and preservational rather than energizing one, it seems clear that English has lost much of its former cultural authority.

In fact, like the wider cultural and political forces themselves, the discipline has entered a condition of chronic instability. The contemporary crisis in English has at least two bases: national and representational. The national element is linked to the decentring of Britain's ('England's') international economic and cultural position. The related representational crisis results from the increasing difficulty of sustaining the illusion of social and economic stability and pluralistic individuality in the face of an accelerating degradation of qualitative difference. There is no longer a major cultural role for the old English within a trans-national network of quantified and repetitive cultural production.[2] It is beyond the power of English literary culture to resolve such massive symbolic and material tensions, especially in that its very marginality in respect of contemporary modes of cultural production and consumption means that it is no longer even assured of the support of state power.

The nature of the discipline's loss of representational focus was dramatically revealed by the 'Cambridge Crisis'. As has been shown, this crisis arose out of perceived challenges to the uniqueness and authenticity of 'English literature'. During the post-war period the identity of the discipline had come to be associated with the reproduction of an educational alternative to 'mass' culture and fictions based upon the uniquely authentic subjectivity that was thought to flow from exposure to an approved corpus of original literary works. Thus, when the functional value of all aspects of English teaching not based upon the preservation of 'great works' was called into question, even radical critics were forced into defending the unique excellence of Cambridge English. The absence of any defence of English on the grounds of its value to democracy by either side in the dispute is very striking indeed.

But, can the objects, institutional mechanisms, and identity of English ever be made compatible with democratic aspirations? The answer to this question depends on what assessment is made of the current condition of the discipline and of the future it is now entering. It seems to me that two contradictory tendencies are currently evident. The first involves a retreat into a museum-like or 'monumental' role with teachers of English as professional curators of a residual 'national cultural heritage'. The second is characterized by attempts to include the conditions underlying the discipline's crisis within its own subject matter – which indeed implies entering into a critical analysis of 'heritage' as such. With respect to this second tendency, it is interesting to note that the goal of much feminist, political, and critical theory might be summed up as a vision of the end of 'literature' in the sense of a privileged cultural domain.[3] Thus, 'the end of literature' means the dismantling of literary fictions as an isolated domain of symbolic experience, and the reintegration of fiction making within other social practices. Such radical work often also involves the recovery of processes of alienation which have been a feature of the construction of 'Great Traditions'. This implies a recognition that even in its pleasures, submission to 'literary' as much as to other fictions can itself be, and in fact has been, alienating. While such a perspective necessarily challenges the inherent 'literary value' associated with a single homogeneous national tradition, it certainly does not imply an end to the activity of fiction production and criticism, but rather its revitalization. In contrast to the posture of cultural submissiveness which an emphasis on 'heritage' tends to impose, such approaches emphasize cultural enablement and active production: indeed, they are often linked to the making of written fictions on both an individual and collective basis.

The future of English studies

This history of the discipline has shown that the constitution of the whole curriculum as a set of subjects determines much of what can and cannot count as 'English'. In other words, important aspects of 'English' are defined by the place of the subject within the system of differences which constitute the curriculum. However, by virtue of the central position that has been allotted to this subject area, 'English' is certain to continue to provide an important locus for current debates on the reconstitution of the curriculum, particularly regarding what are to count as 'communication skills'. For example, the Kingman Committee takes the central purpose of English within the new national curriculum to be the promotion of 'successful communication' through the recognition and accurate use of the rules and conventions relating to varying audiences, contexts, and purposes of language use.[4] However, as Henry Widdowson (a member of the Kingman Committee) points out in his 'Note of reservation', 'what English is on the curriculum *for*, is not really explored here with any rigour'.[5] The consequences are particularly apparent in the refusal to extend a potentially critical concern with varying social and contextual uses to the study of literature. English literature is removed from conflictual social and political history by being defined in the familiar high cultural manner. The Committee sees literature as a body of examples of those aesthetic forms which are said to constitute 'the powerful and splendid history of the best that has been thought and said in our language'.[6] This highly privileged and regulated domain is carefully insulated from the general history of culture:

> In the 1960s and 1970s, there was a desire to bring into the classroom urgent concerns about the relations between language, literature, politics and social conditions. But it has been argued that the result was that English lessons became in some schools no more than the setting for vigorous moral and social discussion, which too often assumed that language was a clear window onto the social world. . . . Too rigid a concern with what is 'relevant' to the lives of young people seems to us to pose the danger of impoverishing not only the young people, but the culture itself, which has to be revitalised by each generation.[7]

One purpose in writing the foregoing history has been precisely to contribute to debates about 'what English is on the curriculum *for*' by clarifying the complex nature and altering role of English studies in modern British education. Through all of the shifting relations which this history has charted, some major referents of the complex term 'English' have remained important. As we move towards the next century they continue to stand as crucial indicators of what English, and indeed formal education as a whole, will and might become. First,

English can be understood as a set of formal institutional mechanisms and curricular frameworks. Second, English is the locus for particular teaching and learning practices: this is the discipline's practical content, its curriculum in action rather than as formally structured. And third, English remains a professional space offering employment, as well as its own documentary field with its own forms of association. Any proposals for change must address all three, and suggest alternative ways in which each might be related to the other.

The striking absence of any defence of the value of English studies for cultural democracy at the time of the Cambridge Crisis has already been mentioned. In effect, at Cambridge, English was understood on all sides purely as a professional study which occupied a central place within what has now come to stand as the 'classical' arts curriculum. That debate concentrated only upon the relative cultural and political value of different critical approaches. Certainly it was not made the occasion for attempts to rewrite or reorientate English within the curriculum, as a cultural practice, or as a profession. Subsequent attempts by the state to re-align education with capitalist enterprise have been less reluctant to engage in rewriting this whole agenda. It is now claimed from the political right that the whole modern curriculum, with English as one of its core elements, is out of step with consumer needs and demands, as well as the demands of the economy.[8]

In some respects this is a familiar enough tactic. This history has charted successive attempts by the state to make education serve 'national interests'. However, we have now entered quite a new phase in which state policy is driven by a more potent and explicit conception of the place of education in promoting *cultural* change. Whereas in the 1920s the Newbolt Committee unsuccessfully proposed English as an instrument of state cultural policy, now it is the government which is elaborating a new cultural policy of its own within which it is seen as the role of education, including English, to propagate an 'enterprise culture'. This at least has the merit of forcing a large-scale reconsideration of the public purpose of formal education upon all concerned. Within the framework of 'enterprise' cultural policy it is the clear purpose of education to reconstruct consciousness of self as prospective worker for the national and international capitalist economy and to sustain conservative patriarchal family life, and indeed to resign the 'unenterprising' to worklessness.

When translated into institutional forms, this is manifested through initiatives based on the Manpower Services Commission and its successors, particularly in secondary and further education. In the higher education sectors the pattern is to shift institutional control from quasi-controlled organizations and local authorities to directly-controlled government funding agencies. What were once marginal Black Paper perspectives have become the basis for a new consensus. Within formal political spheres it is generally accepted that capitalist market forces should be allowed to mould the content of educational provision.

Like other academics, English teachers are now feeling the force of the tendency to bypass professional educational elites in favour of business management initiatives and personnel. Thus far, the new cultural policy has been more successful (in its own terms) in altering course and examination curriculum frameworks than in controlling practical content and professional activity. Increasingly however, practical content as well as curricular and institutional frameworks are also being reassessed by the state. The torrent of abuse unleashed on *Re-Reading English* both in print and on the broadcast media serves to reveal some characteristic responses to such pressures from inside the English studies academic establishment during the mid 1980s.[9] The terrifying calls for the abolition of dissident books and courses, together with reactionary retreats into the narrow professional study of the approved national canon, dramatically enunciates the deep crisis of identity within a profession which feels itself under threat from all sides. Faced by a quite fundamental uncertainty as to what it means to teach something called 'English' today, a major response is to seek the sanctuary of special treatment as custodians of the national culture. Time has revealed the limited protection which such custodianship affords. With the failure of all attempts to reinvigorate a 'traditional' literary-critical consensus has come a complete loss of the sense of cultural function which the combined professional and Leavisian discourses sustained for so long.

In these circumstances, pressures for change are in evidence not only from the political right, but from oppositional forces which, from a very different perspective, also perceive a mismatch between English and the state of contemporary knowledge and modes of cultural organization. One suggestion is to attempt to reconstitute English as the study of 'language' and 'narrative'.[10] However, for such a shift to be meaningful in the context of the history I have discussed above, it is essential that the discipline's underlying 'Englishness' be challenged systematically and effectively rather than simply ignored. Indeed, the inescapable influence of the enterprise cultural policy is itself contributing to wide realization that 'English' has a contingent rather than necessary relation to 'English Literature', and indeed to 'Englishness'. A general recognition of this contingent status is a crucial prerequisite for disciplinary transformation. In fact, in some respects radical change is now rather more likely than at any time in the past. Fortunately, the cultural relativization of Englishness is also one stage in the construction of frameworks, practices, and professional orientations which are capable of being defended as contributions to a democratic rather than 'enterprise' culture. There are a number of trends in this direction, at least at the margins of the discipline and particularly within the lower status educational institutions.[11] Certainly the establishment of new documentary fields (books and journals) and forms of association (networks and conferences) by groups of English teachers and students are encouraging developments. But perhaps the most urgent requirement is the building of links with new 'client' constituencies. To be credible and successful this will necessitate the development of new forms of address, as well as new class, gender, ethnic, and community-based concerns.[12]

Even within the mainstream of the discipline there have been some encouraging recent developments. The now largely autonomous discipline of linguistics has already broken with the essentialist notion of 'the English language'. Here, as in a number of related interdisciplinary fields, the emphasis is upon studying a wide range of modes and relations of linguistic communication and culture more generally. Within the mainstream discipline itself the cultural edifice of 'English literature' has proved more resistant to change, despite some loosening of the links between 'the language' and 'Englishness'. As Edward Said has noted, 'confined to the study of one representational complex, literary critics accept and paradoxically ignore the lines drawn around what they do'.[13] None the less, within a wider range of English departments than in the past, other 'representational complexes' are receiving serious attention. While perhaps still forced by disciplinary inertia or fear of change to focus primarily upon selected literary fictions, many English academics are using the canonized texts only as an instance of the institutionalized channelling of fictions and other forms of discourse. Despite recurrent calls to return exclusively to exegisis of 'the canon of English Literature', there has been some significant movement within as well as beyond the discipline towards the study of the production, formaliz-ation, distribution, and consumption of fictions (including tales, legends, romance, and a host of other kinds of narrative).

Irrespective of questions of subject matter, there are other welcome signs of disciplinary movement in the wider sphere of practical content. Particularly under the influence of feminist analysis, there has been a significant displacement of the central humanistic, masculinized, and Anglo-centred subject around which (as has been shown) most previous disciplinary activity has been orientated and reproduced. This redirection of effort has resulted in a greater understanding of the specific chan-nelling processes by means of which literary fictions have assisted the maintenance of wider, and in many ways alienating or disenabling, cultural relations. There is reason to believe that such current developments have provided English with a basis for generating a non-submissive sense of what might constitute a 'literary education'. It remains to be seen whether actual day to day work within the discipline can effectively address ques-tions of the relations between culture and power, and whether the ways of addressing them can be guided by a critical concern with the enhancement of cultural democracy. On the evidence of the most recent governmental initiatives it seems unlikely that another phase of fundamental reorientation can be avoided by recourse to inherent textual value, plurality of perspective, and disinterested liberal study. If for no other reason than the im-pact of the commercial and institutional imperatives launched in the name of enterprise, there is no longer any option other than to engage with wider debates on cultural democracy and cultural policy. In the light of the current explicit public focus on such issues, it has become impossible any longer to ignore questions about the value of English as a specifically historical, educational, social, and cultural form, rather than simply a self-sustaining practice of worship and hagiography.

It may be that the most positive outcome of this prolonged period of crisis in English (in schools as well as colleges) will prove to be its insistent interrogation of the theoretical, political, and cultural bases of social meaning and value. Now that direct state initiatives have themselves nakedly revealed that cultural values are actively constructed in public spheres well beyond the influence of self-validating realms such as 'Art' and 'English literature', teachers of English are finding it impossible to validate their practice simply by anchoring it to a privileged community of writers and readers. David Sless has argued the urgency of transcending both the 'sharing' and 'transmission' models of communication.[14] As far as English is concerned, the former model is increasingly applied only to the guardianship of shared literary responses among the priests and acolytes of an increasingly unstable interpretative community. As for the rest, the 'transmission' model of the one-way disembodied communication skills increasingly holds sway.

The more exciting, democratic, and indeed humane alternative is a model of communication based on open learning and teaching informed by a sense of differential positions, which enables active involvement in cultural production and change. While institutionally difficult to maintain, this is the only model capable of providing a source of active cultural and political understanding of the distribution of positions from which social meanings and values are negotiated, and the role of fiction making in this process. If, as the evidence seems to suggest, the old subject-centred curriculum is in its twilight days,[15] the pressures to replace basic English teaching with the transmission of communication skills and legitimized 'information' can only increase. One way or another, English studies will be forced to reconstitute itself in terms of discourses on communication and culture. Since culture, communication, and language are at root social forces rather than discrete packages of information and skill, there will always be space for contestation; more perhaps than in the past, given the explicit address by the state to cultural policy. Since not only 'enterprise' but also 'culture' seem destined to become key and controversial terms across teaching in all areas of a newly synthesized curriculum, English can no longer avail itself of the luxury of wilful ignorance of theoretical, cultural, and political implications of these areas of discourse.

It should by now be clear that I take the view that 'English' should be reconstituted as the study of how verbal and written fictions have been produced and used, socially channelled and evaluated, grouped together, given social significance, institutionalized, transformed, repressed, and eliminated. Such studies would be fundamentally relational in that the assumed and projected positions of the individual reader, author, text, and users would all be studied within social semiotic processes, or the making and unmaking of lived meanings. Conceived in this manner, the study of English would no longer primarily serve to produce professional academic masculinized literary critics, or even mature men. Instead, it would be the purpose of such study to develop in students (teachers and taught) a sense of the cultural importance of the ways in which fictions are made, moulded, and channelled, with a view not only to more adequate and active involvement in making use of fictions, but in their production and circulation; and in developing new and more democratic links between modes of consumption, production, and social dissemination.

The history with which this book has been concerned suggests to me that the future of English should be as a cultural or social semiotic study, if it is not to degenerate further into a mixture of professionalized abstraction and the celebration of a falsely harmonious 'heritage'. If it takes the former course, if it develops as the study of how fictions, including literary fictions, have been made and remade; of how this remaking has been linked to, and severed from, various 'English' and other cultural identities – if it can be made to concern itself actively with such issues, the study of English will then provide a creative base for active experiments with cultural production (verbal, visual, and aural) which enhance, improve, and diversify rather than narrow and homogenize our cultural life.

Notes

Introduction: English and popular culture

1 E. J. Hobsbawm and T. Ranger (eds), *The Invention of Tradition*, Cambridge: Cambridge University Press, 1983; R. Colls and P. Dodd (eds), *Englishness: Politics and Culture, 1880–1920*, Beckenham: Croom Helm, 1986.

2 For fuller details of the early history see Brian Doyle 'The hidden history of English studies', in Peter Widdowson (ed.), *Re-Reading English*, London: Methuen, 1982.

3 A contributor to a Congregation debate in 1893 leading to the foundation of the Oxford English School remarked that 'women should be considered, and the second and third-rate men who were to become school masters' (D. J. Palmer, *The Rise of English Studies*, Oxford: Oxford University Press, 1965, 111).

4 For example, Boris Ford (ed.), *The New Pelican Guide to English Literature*, 8 vols, Harmondsworth: Penguin, 1983.

5 Palmer, *op. cit.*; J. M. Newton, 'English Literature at the university: a historical enquiry', unpublished thesis, Clare College, Cambridge, 1963.

6 K. W. S. Garwood, 'The development of the teaching of English, 1830–1920', unpublished thesis, University of Wales, 1954; W. R. Mullins, 'A study of significant changes in the theory of the teaching of English to older pupils in Elementary and Secondary Modern Schools, 1860–1960', unpublished thesis, University of Leicester, 1968.

7 David Shayer, *The Teaching of English in Schools 1900–70*, London: Routledge & Kegan Paul, 1972.

8 J. T. Hodgson, 'Changes in English teaching: institutionalis-ation, transmission and ideology', unpublished thesis, University of London, 1974; Margaret Mathieson, *The Preachers of Culture: A Study of English and its Teachers*, London: Allen & Unwin, 1975.

9 Raymond Williams, 'Literature in society', in H. Schiff (ed.), *Contemporary Approaches to English Studies*, London: Heinemann, 1977.

10 Perry Anderson, 'Components of the national culture', *New Left Review*, 50 (1968), 3–57.

11 Francis Mulhern, *The Moment of 'Scrutiny'*, London: New Left Books, 1979.

12 Pierre Macherey and Etienne Balibar, 'Literature as an ideo-logical form: some marxist propositions', *Oxford Literary Review*, 3, 1 (1978), 4–12; see also: Tony Davies 'Education, ideology and literature', *Red Letters*, 7 (1978), 4–15.

13 For the following discussion, I have drawn extensively upon J. Attali, *Noise: The Political Economy of Music*, Manchester: Manchester University Press, 1985. For some less sympathetic observations on this position see Edward Said, 'Opponents, audiences, constituencies and community', in Hal Foster (ed.), *Postmodern Culture*, London: Pluto Press, 1985.

14 See the entry on 'culture' in Raymond Williams, *Keywords*, London: Fontana, 1976; and Doyle, *op. cit.*

15 See the discussion of 'patronage' in Raymond Williams, *Culture*, London: Fontana, 1981.

16 See Doyle, *op. cit.*

17 Upper-class men were expected to become 'insensibly familiar-ized' to English literature rather than receiving a formal literary education (see Doyle, *op. cit.*).

18 On the historical specialization of 'literature' to 'imaginative writing', see Williams, *Keywords*, *op. cit.*

19 Newbolt Report, *The Teaching of English in England*, London: HMSO, 1921.

20 See Attali, *op. cit.*, 48.

21 See Peter Widdowson '"Literary value" and the reconstruction of criticism', *Literature and History*, 6,2 (Autumn 1980), 138–50.

22 For a more detailed discussion of Hough's perspective, see pp. 116–17.

1 English literature and cultural identities

1 E. J. Hobsbawm, *Industry and Empire*, Harmondsworth: Penguin, 1969, 134; Arthur Marwick, *Britain in a Century of Total War*, Harmondsworth: Penguin, 1968, 20.

2 Hugh Kearney, 'Universities and society in historical perspec-

tive', in R. E. Bell and A. J. Youngson (eds), *Present and Future in Higher Education*, London: Tavistock, 1973.

3   Gareth Stedman Jones, *Outcast London*, Oxford: Clarendon Press, 1971, 242; Peter Keating (ed.), *Into Unknown England*, London: Fontana, 1976, 28.

4   Carol Dyhouse, 'Social Darwinistic ideas and the development of women's education in England, 1880–1920', *History of Education*, 5,1 (1976), 41–58.

5   Joan Burstyn, *Victorian Education and the Ideal of Womanhood*, Beckenham: Croom Helm, 1980, 95.

6   Mirian E. David, *The State, the Family and Education*, London: Routledge & Kegan Paul, 1980, 137.

7   Charles Edwin Vaughan (1854–1922) studied at Balliol College, Oxford, 'when T. H. Green was proclaiming the national work of the universities' (A. N. Shimmin, *The University of Leeds: The First Half Century*, Cambridge: Cambridge University Press, 1954, 123). He was, in fact, strongly influenced by Green (who was his cousin), and by another friend Arnold Toynbee with whom he worked in the East End of London. Having been a teacher at Clifton College, Bristol, for ten years, he moved to Cardiff in 1889 to take the chair of English Language, Literature and History (the title of his chair was changed to 'English Language and Literature' from 1894); then to the chair of English Language and Literature at Newcastle in 1899; and to the chair of English Literature at Leeds in 1904. He was a contributor to the Cambridge History of English Literature, and chairman of the Yorkshire Branch of the English Association, June 1911. (See *Bulletin*, 47, London: English Association, June 1923, hereafter referred to as *Bulletin*.)

8   On the 'settlement movement' see K. S. Inglis, *Churches and the Working Classes in Victorian England*, London: Routledge & Kegan Paul, 1963, ch. 4; on the 'secular mission' see Melvin Richter, *The Politics of Conscience: T. H. Green and his Age*, London: Weidenfeld & Nicholson, 1964, *passim*.

9   For an interesting comparative account of the relations between moral prestige, aesthetic emotion, and cultural mystique in the respective modes of gentlemanly education of English and Chinese elites, see R. H. Wilkinson, 'The gentleman ideal and the maintenance of a political elite', in P. W. Musgrave (ed.), *Sociology, History, and Education*, London: Methuen, 1972.

10   David Kynaston, *King Labour: The British Working Class 1850–1914*, London: Allen & Unwin, 1976. ch. 4.

11   Francis Mulhern, *The Moment of 'Scrutiny'*, London: New Left Books, 1979, 11–14.

12   For an account of the relationship between social administration and the national way of life in the period see Nikolas Rose, 'The psychological complex: mental measurement and social administration', *Ideology and Consciousness*, 5 (Spring 1979), 5–68. Jacques Donzelot, *The Policing of Families*, London: Hutchinson, 1979 provides a more general and structural model; see especially pp. 16–21 and 55–68.

13   Robert G. MacPherson, *The Theory of Higher Education in Nineteenth Century England*, Athens, Georgia: University of Georgia Press, 1959, 116.

14   John Churton Collins, *The Study of English Literature*, London: Macmillan, 1891, 105.

15   *Bulletin*, 8, June 1909.

16   Arthur Quiller-Couch, *On the Art of Writing* (1916), Cambridge: Cambridge University Press, 1928, 139–40.

17   Sheldon Rothblatt, *The Revolution of the Dons*, London: Faber, 1968, 246–7 and *passim*.

18   John Sparrow, *Mark Pattison and the Idea of a University*, Cambridge: Cambridge University Press, 1967, 131.

19   ibid., 129, 146.

20   R. D. Altick, *The English Common Reader*, Chicago: Chicago University Press, 1957, 212.

21   For an analysis of the forms of signification mobilized by the Albert Memorial in Kensington, London, see Michael Eaton, 'Lie back and think of England' in Eileen Phillips (ed.), *The Left and the Erotic*, London: Lawrence & Wishart, 1983.

22   Sheldon Rothblatt, *Tradition and Change in English Liberal Education*, London: Faber, 1976; Ben Knights, *The Idea of the Clericy in the Nineteenth Century*, Cambridge: Cambridge University Press, 1978; and MacPherson, *op. cit.*

23   Michael Sanderson (ed.), *The Universities in the Nineteenth Century*, London: Routledge & Kegan Paul, 1975, 22.

24   Quoted in Shimmin, *op. cit.*, 15.

25   According to Henry Nettleship, by the late 1880s Oxford was being subjected to 'a well-founded national demand' for the introduction of English Language and Literature (see C. H. Firth, *The School of English Language and Literature*, Oxford:Basil Blackwell, 1909, 29.

26   *Regulations for Secondary Schools, 1904*, extract in J. S. Maclure (ed.), *Educational Documents, England and Wales 1816–1967*, Oxford: Oxford University Press, 1968, 158.

27   *The Teaching of English in Secondary Schools*, Board of Education Circular 753, London: HMSO, 1910.

28   David Shayer, *The Teaching of English in Schools 1900–70*, London: Routledge & Kegan Paul, 1972, 35.

29   Altick, *op. cit.*, 184.

30   Brian Doyle, 'The hidden history of English Studies', in Peter Widdowson (ed.), *Re-Reading English*, London: Methuen, 1982.

31   F. W. Moorman (Professor of English Language at Leeds) reported in *Bulletin*, 22, February 1914.

32   C. H. Herford (Professor of English Literature at Manchester) reported in *Bulletin*, 35, September 1918.

33   M. E. Sadler (Vice-Chancellor, University of Leeds) reported in *Bulletin*, 18, November 1912.

34   *Bulletin*, 32, September 1917.

35   J. F. C. Harrison, *Learning and Living 1790–1960*, London: Routledge & Kegan Paul, 1961, 219.

36   ibid., 226.

37   Newbolt Report, *The Teaching of English in England*, London: HMSO, 1921.

38   Richter, *op. cit.*, 135, 360.

39   E. R. Norman, *Church and Society in England 1770–1970*, Oxford: Clarendon Press, 1976, 163–5.

40   Inglis, *op. cit.*, 156.

41   Gerrard Fiennes, quoted in Brian Simon, *Education and the Labour Movement 1870–1920*, London: Lawrence & Wishart, 1965, 83.

42   Simon, *op. cit.*, 82–3; Kynaston, *op. cit.*, 88–9.

43   For a general account of this movement see G. R. Searle, *The Quest for National Efficiency: A Study in British Politics and British Political Thought 1899–1914*, Oxford: Blackwell, 1971; see also Simon, *op. cit.*, 175.

44   Simon, *op. cit.*, 79–80.

45   ibid., 79.

46   ibid., 170.

47   ibid., 175.

48   Nowell Smith, *The Origins and History of the Association*, London: English Association, 1942, 5.

49   *Bulletin*, 3, February 1908.

50   *Bulletin*, 10, February 1910.

51   *Bulletin*, 11, June 1910.

52   *Bulletin*, 37, April 1919; and *Bulletin*, 38, September 1919.

53   *Bulletin*, 19, February 1913.

54   Smith, *op. cit.*, 6–7.

55   W. J. Courthope's address to the AGM of the Association, as reported in *Bulletin*, 7, February 1909. He was author of the influential *History of English Poetry* (see Quiller-Couch, *op. cit.*). Compare Courthope's remarks with the claim made by Collins

in 1891 that 'it is the privilege of Art and Letters to bring us into contact with the aristocrats of our race' (Collins, *op. cit.*, 66). Courthope was one of the 'witnesses' called upon by Collins to support his case for the introduction of English Language and Literature at Oxford.

56 See the reports on H. Montagu Butler's speech in *Bulletin*, 3, January 1908, and W. Boyd's paper on 'The mental differences between the primary and the secondary pupil, and their bearings on the English teacher's work', in *Bulletin*, 10, February 1910.

57 J. H. Fowler of Clifton College, Bristol, and a member of the original executive committee of the Association, moved the following motion at the Federal Conference of Education in London in 1907: 'That this Conference urges the importance of the study of the English language and literature as an essential part of School Training on the grounds of practical utility, enlightened patriotism, and the human ideal in education' (*Bulletin*, 1, July 1907).

58 *Bulletin*, 22, February 1914.

59 *Bulletin*, 1, July 1907.

60 *Bulletin*, 35, September 1918.

61 *Bulletin*, 36, January 1919.

62 *Bulletin*, 16, February 1912.

63 *Bulletin*, 19, February 1913; Bailey's contribution to the Newbolt Report is discussed in R. W. Chambers's pamphlet which also includes a rejoinder by Bailey.

64 *Bulletin*, 19, February 1913.

65 John Bailey, *A Question of Taste*, London: English Association, pamphlet 65, 1926, 7.

66 ibid., 19.

67 *Bulletin*, 35, September 1918.

68 *Bulletin*, 7, February 1909.

69 ibid.

70 ibid.

71 ibid.

72 *Bulletin*, 19, February 1913; *Bulletin*, 22, February 1914.

73 L. T. Hobhouse, *Liberalism*, quoted by Searle, *op. cit.*, 256.

74 *Bulletin*, 7, February 1909.

75 J. W. Mackail, as reported in *Bulletin*, 3, February 1908.

76 *Bulletin*, 3, February 1908.

77 ibid.

78 *Bulletin*, 6, November 1908; *Bulletin*, 8, June 1909.

79 A. M. Williams, Principal of Glasgow Training College, as reported in *Bulletin*, 10, February 1910.

2   English, the state, and cultural policy

1   Iain Wright, 'On the social responsibility of literature', *THES*, 12 November 1976, 17; see also Margaret Mathieson, *The Preachers of Culture: A Study of English and its Teachers*, London: Allen & Unwin, 1975, 69–84.

2   Patrick Parrinder, 'Sermons, pseudo-science and critical discourse', *Studies in Higher Education*, 4,1 (1979), 5–6; Chris Baldick, *The Social Mission of English Criticism 1848–1932*, Oxford: Basil Blackwell, 1983, 143.

3   Carole Snee, 'Period studies and the place of criticsm', in Peter Widdowson (ed.), *Re-Reading English: Essays on Literature and Criticism in Higher Education*, London: Methuen, 1982, 168.

4   *Bulletin*, 19, February 1913, 7.

5   Nicholas M. Pearson, *The State and Visual Arts: A Discussion of State Intervention in the Visual Arts in Britain 1760–1981*, Milton Keynes: Open University Press, 1982, 1.

6   ibid., 47–50.

7   Arthur Marwick, *Britain in a Century of Total War*, Harmondsworth: Penguin, 1970, 182; A. J. P. Taylor, *English History 1914–1945*, Oxford: Clarendon Press, 1965, 185–6.

8   Pearson, *op. cit.*, 47.

9   Marwick, *op. cit.*, ch. 3.

10   Keith Middlemas, *Politics in Industrial Society: The Experience of the British System since 1911*, London: Andre Deutsch, 1979, 371.

11   Taylor, *op. cit.*, 176.

12   See W. H. G. Armytage, *Civic Universities: Aspects of a British Tradition*, London: Ernest Benn, 1955, 267 on Ernest Barker, and also Barker's own *National Character and the Factors in its Formation*, London: Methuen, 1927, reprinted 1948; George Sampson, *English for the English: a Chapter on National Education*, Cambridge: Cambridge University Press, 1921, reprinted 1926, and Taylor, *op. cit.*, 173–4.

13   Newbolt Report, *The Teaching of English in England*, London: HMSO, 1921, para. 1, p. 4. All further references to the Report are given in the text as paragraph numbers followed by page references.

14   Robert Colls and Philip Dodd, 'Representing the nation – British documentary film 1930–45', *Screen*, 26,1 (1985), 21–33.

15   Raymond Williams, 'The Bloomsbury fraction', in *Problems in Materialism and Culture*, London: Verso, 1980, 155.

3 English as a masculine profession

1 G. S. Gordon, 'The discipline of letters', Oxford inaugural lecture, 1923; R. W. Chambers, *The Teaching of English in the Universities of England*, London: English Association, 1922; R. W. Chambers, *Concerning Certain Great Teachers of the English Language*, London: Arnold, 1925.

2 C. D. Burns, *A Short History of Birkbeck College*, London: London University Press, 1924, 123.

3 T. E. B. Howarth, *Cambridge Between the Wars*, London: Collins, 1978, 84.

4 Brian Simon, *Education and the Labour Movement 1870–1920*, London: Lawrence & Wishart, 1965, 343.

5 ibid.

6 J. Dover Wilson, *Milestones on the Dover Road*, London: Faber, 1969.

7 Howarth, *op. cit.*, 86; D. J. Palmer, *The Rise of English Studies*, Oxford: Oxford University Press, 1965, 127.

8 In what follows I have drawn extensively upon J. Hearn, *The Gender of Oppression*, Brighton: Wheatsheaf, 1987, and J. Hearn and W. Parkin, *'Sex' at 'Work': The Power and Paradox of Organisation Sexuality*, Brighton: Wheatsheaf, 1987.

9 See F. L. Lucas, 'English literature', in Harold Wright (ed.), *University Studies Cambridge 1933*, Cambridge: Ivor Nicholson & Watson, 1933; Basil Willey, *Cambridge and Other Memories 1920 –53*, London: Chatto & Windus, 1968.

10 Hearn, *op. cit.*

11 See T. Lovell, *Consuming Fiction*, London: Verso, 1987, 144–5.

12 Wilson, *op. cit.*, 154,174.

13 Members of the initial panel were: A. C. Bradley, E. K. Chambers, R. W. Chambers, R. W. Chapman, H. B. Charlton, O. Elton, G. Gordon, W. W. Greg, H. Grierson, C. H. Herford, A. Mawer, E. Morley, H. Newbolt, Allardyce Nicoll, A. W. Pollard, A. N. Reed, E. de Selincourt, P. Simpson, C. Spurgeon, J. Dover Wilson, and H. C. Wyld.

14 *The Review of English Studies* II, 6 (1926), 242 (hereafter *Review*); when not identified in the text, the names of individual authors are placed within brackets in the appropriate notes.

15 *Review*, III,12 (1927), 439–9.

16 ibid., 430.

17 ibid., 431.

18 ibid., 437.

19 *Review*, VII, 25 (1931), 95 (A. C. Healing).

20 See, for example, *Review*, XI, 43 (1935), 482 (G. B. Harrison) and XIII, 44 (1937), (Catherine M. Maclean).

21 *Review*, VI, 21 (1930), 77–8.
22 See *Review*, XI, 41 (1935), 1 (A. Lytton Sells).
23 *Review*, IX, 35 (1933), 326.
24 *Review*, I, 3 (1925), 374, 359 (J. Dover Wilson).
25 *Review*, II, 7 (1926), 286, 290 (A. S. Collins).
26 *Review*, XI, 41 (1935), 101 (Vivian de Sola Pinto).
27 *Review*, IX, 33 (1933), 101.
28 ibid., 100.
29 Francis Mulhern, *The Moment of 'Scrutiny'*, London: New Left Books, 1979, 157–8.
30 *Review*, I, 2 (1925), 221 (obituary).
31 *Review*, VI, 24 (1930), 453 (obituary).
32 ibid.
33 *Review*, VIII, 27 (1931), 341 (G. C. Moore Smith).
34 *Review*, II, 7 (1926), 318–21 (obituary).
35 *Review*, VII, 26 (1931), 227–8.
36 *Review*, I, 1 (1925), 39.
37 *Review*, I, 4 (1925), 385, 390 (John S. Smart).
38 *Review*, VI, 21 (1930), 52 (P. L. Carver).
39 *Review*, I, 4 (1925), 498 (Edith J. Morley).
40 *Review*, III, 9 (1927), 104 (G. B. Harrison).
41 *Review*, IX, 34 (1933), 147 (Helen L. Gardner).
42 *Review*, I, 1 (1925), 2.
43 *Review*, VII, 26 (1931), 217.
44 *Review*, XVI, 61 (1940), 116–17.
45 *Review*, XVI, 63 (1940), 260.
46 *Review*, VII, 25 (1931), 111–12.
47 See David Shayer, *The Teaching of English in Schools 1900–70*, London: Routledge & Kegan Paul, 1972, 126, 167.
48 Stephen Potter, *The Muse in Chains: A Study in Education*, London: Jonathan Cape, 1937, 36.
49 See, for example, *Review*, VI, 24 (1930), 493 ('L.F.').
50 *Review*, IX, 34 (1933), 228 (John Brett).
51 *Review*, XII, 47 (1936), 367–8.
52 *Review*, VI, 23 (1930), 368 (Vivian de Sola Pinto).
53 *Review*, XII, 47 (1936), 494.
54 *Review*, XIV, 54 (1938), 245.
55 *Review*, I, 1 (1925), 1–3.
56 ibid., 118–19.
57 *Review*, IV, 14 (1928), 224–5.
58 *Review*, II, 5 (1926), 63.
59 *Review*, VI, 21 (1930), 30.
60 ibid., 2.
61 *Review*, IX, 35 (1933), 323.

62   *Review*, XI, 42 (1935), 240–1.
63   C. S. Lewis quoted in *Review*, XVI, 61 (1940), 112 (J. B. Leishman).
64   *Review*, XVI, 62 (1946), 245–6 (Harold Williams).
65   *Review*, I, 1 (1925), 1.
66   *Review*, III, 9 (1925), 105.
67   ibid.
68   *Review*, IV, 15 (1928), 349.
69   *Review*, IV, 13 (1928), 121.
70   *Review*, X, 37 (1934), 113 (B. E. C. Davis).
71   *Review*, XVI, 63 (1940), 261 (G. B. Harrison).
72   *Review*, VII, 26 (1931), 217–19.
73   ibid.
74   Quoted by Terence J. Johnson, *Professions and Power*, London: Macmillan, 1972, 14.
75   *Review*, I, 1 (1925), 60–1.
76   *Review*, I, 2 (1925), 181.
77   *Review*, I, 3 (1925), 308.
78   *Review*, I, 4 (1925), 385, 390 (John S. Smart).
79   *Review*, II, 5 (1926), 50.
80   *Review*, XI, 43 (1935), 355.
81   *Review*, I, 3 (1925), 366 (Edith J. Morley).
82   Johnson, *op. cit.*, 56.
83   *Review*, IV, 14 (1928), 244.
84   *Review*, XI, 41 (1935), 89 (Alice Walker).
85   *Review*, VI, 21 (1930), 94.
86   *Review*, XIII, 49 (1937), 104–6.
87   *Review*, XVI, 61 (1940), 84.
88   *Review*, XIII, 52 (1937), 477.
89   *Review*, XIV, 54 (1938), 228 (Ernest A. Baker).
90   *Review*, I, 4 (1925), 478 (W. W. Greg).
91   *Review*, XI, 43 (1935), 361 (R. W. King).
92   See F. R. Leavis, *Education and the University: A Sketch for an 'English School'* (1943), London: Chatto & Windus, 1965, 74–6.
93   Mulhern, *op. cit.*, *passim*.
94   David Daiches, 'The place of English Studies in the Sussex scheme', in David Daiches (ed.), *The Idea of a New University*, London: Andre Deutsch, 1964, 85.
95   Howarth, *op. cit.*, 166.
96   Lucas, *op. cit.*, 275, 290.
97   *Review*, XI, 44 (1935), 494–6.
98   Francis Mulhern, 'Intelligentsia regroups to fight the British crisis', *THES*, 22 May 1981, 11–12.
99   ibid.

100 Mulhern, *The Moment of 'Scrutiny'*, *op. cit.*, 40.
101 ibid.
102 John Gross, *The Rise and Fall of the Man of Letters: Aspects of English Literary Life since 1800*, Harmondsworth: Penguin, 1973, 209.
103 G. L. Bickersteth, 'English studies at the university', *Aberdeen University Review*, March 1939, 116–24.
104 ibid.
105 ibid., 118.
106 ibid., 119.
107 ibid., 121–2.
108 ibid., 122.

4 English, culture, and democracy

1 F. R. Leavis, *Education and the University: A Sketch for an 'English School'* (1943), London: Chatto & Windus, 1965.
2 ibid., 7–8.
3 ibid., 17.
4 ibid., 16.
5 ibid., 8.
6 ibid., 55.
7 ibid., 51.
8 ibid., 29.
9 ibid., 34.
10 ibid., 42.
11 ibid., 60, 48.
12 ibid., 49.
13 ibid., 56.
14 ibid., 70–3.
15 James Mountford, *Keele: An Historical Critique*, London: Routledge & Kegan Paul, 1972, 114.
16 ibid., 139–40.
17 ibid., 124–7.
18 Louis Arnaud Reid, 'The nature and justification of an "Arts" education', *Universities Quarterly*, 3, 1 (1948), 498.
19 ibid., 504.
20 ibid., 497–8.
21 See Arthur Marwick, *Britain in a Century of Total War*, Harmondsworth: Penguin, 1970, 383; University Grants Committee, *Statistics of Education*, vol. 6: *Universities*, London: HMSO, 1971; Keith Middlemas, *Politics in Industrial Society: The Experience of the British System since 1911*, London: Andre Deutsch, 1979, 36n.

22   Reid, *op. cit.*, 497.

23   ibid., 500–1, 502.

24   Vivien de Sola Pinto, 'Notes on the School of English studies in the University of Nottingham', *Universities Quarterly*, 5, 3 (1951), 225–31.

25   ibid. 225–7.

26   A. C. Wood, *A History of University College, Nottingham 1881–1948*, Oxford: Basil Blackwell, 1953, 145.

27   James Kinsley, *English Studies in the University*, inaugural lecture, Swansea: University College, 1954, 3.

28   ibid., 8.

29   ibid., 21.

30   James Kinsley, 'English Studies at Nottingham', *Critical Survey*, 1, 2 (1963), 119.

31   L. C. Knights, 'The university teaching of English and History: a plea for correlation', in L. C. Knights, *Explorations: Essays in Criticism Mainly on the Literature of the Seventeenth Century*, London: Chatto & Windus, 1946, 191.

32   ibid., 186–7, 190.

33   ibid., 187.

34   ibid., 190, 191.

35   ibid., 192–3, 195.

36   Raymond Williams, *Politics and Letters*, London: New Left Books, 1979, 72, 66.

37   D. G. James, 'The teaching of English in universities', *Universities Quarterly*, 5, 3 (1951), 233.

38   ibid.

39   John Butt, 'English at the universities 1901–1951', *Universities Quarterly*, 5, 3 (1951), 220, 223.

40   Brian Doyle, 'Fictions and ideology 1920–1940', unpublished dissertation, Thames Polytechnic, London, 1978.

41   James, *op. cit.*, 235.

42   ibid., 235–6, 237–8.

43   Helen Gardner, 'The academic study of English literature', *Critical Quarterly*, 1, ii (1959), 107.

44   ibid., 108, 111.

45   M. J. Collie, 'Value and the teaching of literature', *Universities Quarterly*, 12 (1958), 181.

46   ibid., 182.

47   ibid., 181.

48   ibid., 182, 184–5.

49   C. P. Snow, *The Two Cultures and the Scientific Revolution*, Cambridge: Cambridge University Press, 1959.

50   F. R. Leavis, 'Two cultures? The significance of C. P. Snow',

Spectator, 9 March 1962; see Francis Mulhern, *The Moment of 'Scrutiny'*, London: New Left Books, 1979, 305n.

51 Snow, *op. cit.*, 2, 38, 6–8ff.

52 Colin Gordon, *The Foundation of the University of Salford*, Altringham: Sherratt, 1975, 144.

53 Raymond Chapman, 'The place of English literature in modern education', *Higher Education Journal*, 8, 3 (1951), 17–19.

54 D. S. Brewer, 'English in the University III: Language and Literature', *Essays in criticism*, 11, iii (1961), 254.

55 F. W. Bateson, 'Organs of critical opinion: 1   *The Review of English Studies, Essays on Criticism*, VI, 2 (1956), 190–201, reprinted in F. W. Bateson (ed.), *Essays in Critical Dissent*, London: Longman, 1972, 67.

56 Williams, *op. cit.*, 85 (editors' question).

57 F. W. Bateson, 'Oxford English', *New Statesman* 7 December 1965, 973–4, reprinted in Bateson, *Essays, op. cit.*, 187.

58 F. W. Bateson, 'English in the University I: the English school in a democracy', *Essays in Criticism*, IX, 3 (1959), 265–86, reprinted in Bateson, *Essays, op. cit.*, 182.

59 ibid., 180.

60 Bateson, *Essays, op. cit.*, 80, 192.

61 Bateson, 'English in the University I', *op. cit.*, 179; Bateson, *Essays, op. cit.*, 12.

62 Bateson, *Essays, op. cit.*, 197.

63 Bateson, 'English in the University I', *op. cit.*, 182.

64 Bateson, *Essays, op. cit.*, 78.

65 ibid., 75.

66 ibid., XVII, 'I should say they [the scientists] naturally had the future in their bones' (Snow, *op. cit.*, 10).

67 Bateson, 'English in the University I', *op. cit.*, 171, 169, 165.

68 ibid., 170–1.

69 ibid., 167, 182.

70 ibid., 167.

71 Interview with Terence Hawkes.

72 Klaus Boehm (ed.), *University Choice*, Harmondsworth: Penguin, 1966, 7. This was also confirmed in personal interviews.

73 ibid., 9.

74 Philip Brockbank, 'English', in Boehm *op. cit.*, 137.

75 W. D. Emrys Evans, 'Survey of the surveys', *Critical Survey*, 3, 3 (1967), 184.

76 Brockbank, *op. cit.*, 149–50.

77 Robbins Report, *Higher Education*, London: HMSO, 1963, 4–5.

78 ibid., 47, 7.

79   Albert E. Sloman, *A University in the Making*, 1963 Reith Lectures, London: BBC, 1964, 11, 10.

80   John Butt, 'Comment on new universities', *Critical Survey*, 1, 2 (1963), 115–16.

81   D. J. Palmer, *The Rise of English Studies*, Oxford: Oxford University Press, 1965, 162–4.

82   Kinsley, *English Studies*, 1954, *op. cit.*, 11.

83   Daiches, 'The place of English studies in the Sussex scheme', in Daiches (ed.), 1964, 87.

84   ibid., 99.

85   Richard Hoggart, 'English in extra-mural education', *Universities Quarterly*, 5, 3 (1951), 255.

86   Allan Rodway and Mark Roberts, 'English in the University II: "practical criticism" in principle and practice', *Essays in Criticism*, X, 1 (1960), 13.

87   Colin Falck, 'Liberal studies', *TLS*, 25 July 1968, 797–8.

88   Richard Hoggart, *The Uses of Literacy: Aspects of Working-Class Life with Special Reference to Publications and Entertainments* (1957), Harmondsworth: Penguin, 1962, 13.

89   T. R. Barnes, 'English as a specialist discipline', *Journal of Education*, 89, 1054 (1957).

90   Falck, *op. cit.*, 798.

91   Richard Hoggart, 'Why I value literature', in George Steiner et al., *The Critical Moment*, London: Faber, 1964, 33.

92   Richard Hoggart, 'The literary imagination and the study of society', CCCS Occasional Paper no. 3, University of Birmingham, 1967, 3.

93   Richard Hoggart, 'Contemporary cultural studies: an approach to the study of literature and society', CCCS Occasional Paper no. 6, University of Birmingham, 1969, 19.

94   Hoggart, 'The literary imagination', *op. cit.*, 9.

95   See, for example, Knights, 'The university teaching of English and History', *op. cit.*, 194n and Chapman, *op. cit.*, 21.

96   Elizabeth Owen and John Oakley, ' "English" and the Council for National Academic Awards', in Peter Widdowson (ed.), *Re-Reading English*, London: Methuen, 1982.

97   Williams, *op. cit.*, 85.

98   F. R. Leavis, *English Literature in Our Time and the University: The Clark Lectures 1967*, London: Chatto & Windus, 1969, 1.

99   George Steiner, 'Humane literacy', in George Steiner et al., *The Critical Moment*, London: Faber, 1964, 23.

100 J. H. Plumb (ed.), *Crisis in the Humanities*, Harmondsworth: Penguin, 1964, 10.

101   Graham Hough, 'Crisis in literary education', in Plumb *op. cit.*, 97–9.

102   ibid., 100, 82–3.

103   Graham Hough, 'The function of imagination', in Steiner et al., *op. cit.*, 102.

104   ibid., 108–9.

105   Hough, 'Crisis', *op. cit.*, 84.

106   'Mincing words', *TLS*, 25 July 1968, 767.

107   W. W. Robson, 'The future of English Studies', *TLS* 25 July 1968, 773–4.

108   C. B. Cox and A. E. Dyson, 'Word in the desert', *Critical Quarterly*, 10, 1/2 (1968), 1–2.

109   ibid., 7.

110   A. E. Dyson, 'Literature – in the younger universities', *Critical Quarterly*, 1, ii (1959), 119.

111   ibid., 117, 121, 118.

112   G. H. Bantock, 'Why teach literature: in the training college', *Critical Quarterly*, 1, i (1959), 50.

113   G. H. Bantock, *The Implications of Literacy: An Inaugural Lecture Delivered in the University of Leicester 19 October 1965*, Leicester: Leicester University Press, 1966, 16.

114   ibid., 18, 18–19, 21.

115   T. R. Henn, 'The shape of English teaching', in Peter Bander (ed.), *Looking Forward to the Seventies*, London: Colin Smythe, 1968, 319–21.

116   C. B. Cox and A. E. Dyson, *Fight for Education: A Black Paper*; *Black Paper Two: The Crisis in Education*; *Black Paper Three: Goodbye Mr. Short*, Critical Quarterly Society, 1969; 1970; 1970; C. B. Cox and Rhodes Boyson, *Black Paper 1975: The Fight for Education*, London: Dent, 1975 and C. B. Cox and Rhodes Boyson, *Black Paper 1977*, London: Temple Smith, 1977. See also Centre for Contemporary Cultural Studies, *Unpopular Education: Schooling and Social Democracy since 1944*, London: Hutchinson, 1981, ch. 9.

117   Bantock, *The Implications of Literacy*, *op. cit.*, 19.

118   Michael Paffard, *Thinking About English*, London: Ward Lock, 1978, 65.

119   ibid., 52, 64, 86.

120   F. R. Leavis, *The Living Principle: English as a Discipline of Thought*, London: Chatto & Windus, 1975, 11.

121   *TLS*, 4 February to 14 April 1972: 9 weekly articles.

122   *TLS*, 14 February 1972, 411. This was confirmed by a number of English teachers in personal interviews.

123   Keith Brown and Christophe Campos, 'Literature studies and

English literature – the logic of success', *University Quarterly*, 26,1 (1971), 41.

124   ibid., 54.

125   Pat Rogers, *The Courage to be Literary*, Winchester: King Alfred's College, 1979, 7, and Parrinder, *op. cit.*, 11 offer just two such examples. For a history written in such terms, see John Fekete, *The Critical Twilight: Explorations in the Ideology of Anglo-American Literary Theory from Eliot to McLuhan*, London: Routledge & Kegan Paul, 1978.

126   Graham Hough, 'Criticism as a humanist discipline', in Malcolm Bradbury and David Palmer (eds), *Contemporary Criticism*, London: Edward Arnold, 1970, 50.

127   Peter Widdowson, 'Literature in society' in David Craig and Margot Heineman (eds), *Experiments in English Teaching*, London: Edward Arnold, 1976, 135.

128   Rogers, *op. cit.*, 17.

129   Once again the work of Raymond Williams is exceptional. However, even in recent years he has given little attention to teaching practices and institutional arrangements.

130   Raymond Cowell, *The Critical Enterprise: English Studies in Higher Education*, London: Allen & Unwin, 1975, 70.

131   Hilda Schiff (ed.), *Contemporary Approaches to English Studies*, London: Heinemann, 1977, 6.

132   ibid., 3. One of the most useful examples is considered below, pp. 126–8, i.e. Tony Davies, 'Common sense and critical practice: teaching literature' in Widdowson (ed.), *Re-Reading English*, *op. cit.*

133   Parrinder, *op. cit.*, 11.

134   Denis Donoghue quoted by Garry Watson, *The Leavises, the 'Social' and the Left*, Swansea: Brynmill, 1977, 118–19.

135   Frank Kermode quoted in ibid., 127.

136   As Terry Eagleton has observed, in *Literary Theory*, Oxford: Basil Blackwell, 1983, 198–9.

137   *TLS*, 3 March 1972, 251.

138   Rogers, *op. cit.*, 6–7.

139   ibid., 7, 3–4.

140   ibid., 4, 6.

141   Davies, 'Common sense', *op. cit.*, 38.

142   ibid., 34.

143   Barbara Hardy, 'The teaching of literature in the university', *English in Education*, Spring 1973, 34.

144   ibid., 35.

145   Davies, 'Common sense', *op. cit.*, 37.

146   Hardy, *op. cit.*, 35.

147 John Broadbent, 'New university English' in Craig and Heineman, *op. cit.*

148 ibid., 33, 37, 38.

149 Hardy, *op. cit.*, 38.

150 Davies, 'Common sense', *op. cit.*, 34.

151 ibid., 37.

152 Hardy, *op. cit.*, 33.

153 See *TLS*, 24 March 1972, 331.

154 ibid., 332.

155 Harold F. Brooks, 'Cambridge debate', letter in *THES*, 13 March 1981, 26.

156 'Dons in bitter row over English literary policy', *Guardian*, 16 January 1981, 12.

157 Mervyn Jones, 'The Oxbridge malaise', *Guardian*, 14 February 1981, 9.

158 'New post offer to don in English dispute', *Guardian*, 30 May 1981, 1.

159 'New post for MacCabe', *THES*, 5 June 1981, 2.

160 'Strathclyde structure suits MacCabe', *THES*, 26 June 1981, 3; Terry Eagleton, 'The Cambridge Crisis', *Time Out*, 6 February 1981, 5.

161 'Cambridge scholars wage literal warfare', *THES*, 23 January 1981, 3.

162 ibid.

163 *TLS*, 25 February 1972, 215.

164 ibid.

165 ibid.

166 'The world this weekend', BBC Radio 4, 25 January 1981.

167 *TLS*, 25 February 1972, 216.

168 Jones, *op. cit.*, 9.

169 For a very instructive analysis of the significance of the Cambridge English 'crisis' see Francis Mulhern, 'The Cambridge affair', *Marxism Today*, 25, 3 (1981), 27–8.

170 'The world this weekend', *op. cit.*

Conclusion: Fiction, culture and society

1 See Graham Hough, 'The turn of the native', *TLS*, 4 March 1983, 217.

2 For a discussion of this trans-national cultural economy see J. Attali, *Noise: The Political Economy of Music*, Manchester: Manchester University Press, 1985, Chapter 4.

3 See J. Batsleer, T. Davies, R. O'Rourke and C. Weedon,

Rewriting English: Cultural Politics of Gender and Class, London: Methuen, 1985, 11–12, and Chapter 8.

4   The Kingman Committee, *Report of the Committee of Inquiry into the Teaching of English Language*, London: HMSO, 1988, paragraph 11, p. 3.

5   ibid., p. 77.

6   ibid., paragraph 22, p. 11.

7   ibid., paragraph 24, p. 12; paragraph 22, p. 11.

8   A. Wood, 'To provide for the nation', *Royal Society of Arts News*, 8, summer 1985, 7.

9   Peter Widdowson (ed.), *Re-Reading English*, London: Methuen, 1982; T. Davies, 'Damning the tides: the new English and the reviewers', in M. Green (ed.), *English and Cultural Studies: Broadening the Context*, London: John Murray, 1987.

10 Colin MacCabe, 'The sunset of the British Empire', *Guardian*, 28 February 1983, 9.

11 I am thinking of courses in Humanities, and particularly in Communication, Media, and Cultural Studies.

12 For further information on meetings, conferences, publications etc. see journals such as *Literature Teaching Politics*, *Literature and History*, and *Red Letters*. On cultural democracy see Owen Kelly, *Community, Art and the State*, London: Comedia, 1984; P. Gilroy, *There Ain't No Black in the Union Jack*, London, Hutchinson: 1987; and K. Owusu, *The Struggle for Black Arts in Britain*, London: Comedia, 1985.

13 Edward Said, 'Opponents, audiences, constituencies and community', in Hal Foster (ed.), *Postmodern Culture*, London: Pluto Press, 1985, 153.

14 D. Sless, *In Search of Semiotics*, Beckenham, Croom Helm, 1986; on 'positions' see also A. Durant, *Conditions of Music*, London: Macmillan, 1984.

15 D. Lusted, 'English teaching and media education: culture and the curriculum', in Green (ed.), *op. cit.*

References

Anthony Adams and John Pearce, *Every English Teacher: A Guide to English Teaching for the Non-specialist*, Oxford: Oxford University Press, 1974.

R. D. Altick, *The English Common Reader: A Social History of the Mass Reading Public*, Chicago: Chicago University Press, 1957.

Perry Anderson, 'Components of the national culture', *New Left Review*, 50 (1968), 3–57.

W. H. G. Armytage, *Civic Universities: Aspects of a British Tradition*, London: Ernest Benn, 1955.

J. Attali, *Noise: The Political Economy of Music*, Manchester: Manchester University Press, 1985.

John Bailey, *A Question of Taste*, London: The English Association, 1926, pamphlet no. 65.

Chris Baldick, *The Social Mission of English Criticism 1848–1932*, Oxford: Basil Blackwell, 1983.

Renée Balibar, *Les Francais fictifs: le Rapport des styles litteraires au Francais National*, Paris: Hachette, 1974.

—— 'An example of literary work in France: George Sand's "La Mare au Diable"/"The Devil's Pool" of 1846', in F. Barker, J. Coombes, P. Hulme, C. Mercer, and D. Mussel White (eds), *1848: The Sociology of Literature*, Colchester: University of Essex, 1978, 27–46.

Renée Balibar and D. Lapore, *Le Francais National: Politique et practique de la langue national sur la Revolution*, Paris: Hachette, 1974.

Peter Bander, ed., *Looking Forward to the Seventies: A Blueprint for Education in the Next Decade*, London: Colin Smythe, 1968.

G. H. Bantock, 'Why teach literature: in the training college', *Critical Quarterly*, 1, i (1959), 50–3.

——*The Implications of Literacy: An Inaugural Lecture delivered in the University of Leicester 19 October 1965*, Leicester: Leicester University Press, 1966.

Ernest Barker, *National Character and the Factors in its Formation*, London: Methuen, 1927, reprinted 1948.

T. R. Barnes, 'English as a specialist discipline', *Journal of Education*, 89, 1054 (1957), 208–12.

F. W. Bateson, 'Organs of critical opinion: 1 *The Review of English Studies*', *Essays in Criticism*, VI, 2 (1956), 190–201, reprinted in F. W. Bateson, ed., *Essays in Critical Dissent*, London: Longman, 1972.

——'English in the University I: the English school in a democracy', *Essays in Criticism*, IX, 3 (1959), 265–86, reprinted in F. W. Bateson, ed., *Essays in Critical Dissent*, London: Longman, 1972.

——'Oxford English', *New Statesman*, 17 December 1965, 973–4.

——*Essays in Critical Dissent*, London: Longman, 1972.

Janet Batsleer, Tony Davies, Rebecca O'Rourke, and Chris Weedon, *Rewriting English: Cultural Politics of Gender and Class*, London: Methuen, 1985.

BBC Radio 4, 'The world this weekend', 25 January 1981.

R. E. Bell and A. J. Youngson, eds, *Present and Future in Higher Education*, London: Tavistock, 1973.

Tony Bennett, *Formalism and Marxism*, London: Methuen, 1979.

Basil Bernstein, 'On the classification and framing of educational knowledge', *Class, Codes and Control*, vol. 31, *Towards a Theory of Educational Transmissions*, London: Routledge & Kegan Paul, 1971, reprinted 1977.

G. L. Bickersteth, 'English studies at the university', *Aberdeen University Review*, March 1939, 116–24.

Harry Blamires, *A Short History of English Literature*, London: Methuen, 1974.

Board of Education, *The Teaching of English in Secondary Schools* (1906), London: HMSO, expanded 1910.

Klaus Boehm, ed., *University Choice*, Harmondsworth: Penguin, 1966.

Malcolm Bradbury, *The Social Context of Modern English Literature*, Oxford: Basil Blackwell, 1971.

Malcolm Bradbury and David Palmer, eds, *Contemporary Criticism* (Stratford-upon-Avon Studies, 12), London: Edward Arnold, 1970.

D. S. Brewer, 'English in the University III: Language and Literature', *Essays in Criticism*, II, iii (1961), 243–63.

John Broadbent, 'New university English', in David Craig and Margot Heineman, eds, *Experiments in English Teaching*, London: Edward Arnold, 1976.

Philip Brockbank, 'English', in Klaus Boehm ed., *University Choice*, Harmondsworth: Penguin, 1966.

Harold F. Brooks, 'Cambridge debate' (letter), *THES*, 13 March 1981, 26.

Keith Brown and Christophe Campos, 'Literature studies and English literature – the logic of success', *Universities Quarterly*, 26, 1 (1971), 41–65.

C. D. Burns, *A Short History of Birkbeck College*, London: London University Press, 1924.

Joan N. Burstyn, *Victorian Education and the Ideal of Womanhood*, Beckenham: Croom Helm, 1980.

John Butt, 'English at the universities 1901–1951', *Universities Quarterly*, 5, 3 (1951), 218–24.

John Butt, 'Comment on new universities', *Critical Survey*, 1, 2, (1963), 115–16.

Centre for Contemporary Cultural Studies, *Unpopular Education: Schooling and Social Democracy in England since 1944*, London: Hutchinson, 1981.

R. W. Chambers, *The Teaching of English in the Universities of England*, London: English Association, 1922, Pamphlet no. 53.

R. W. Chambers, *Concerning Certain Great Teachers of the English Language: An Inaugural Lecture Delivered in University College London*, London: Edward Arnold, 1925.

Raymond Chapman, 'The place of English literature in modern education', *Higher Education Journal*, 8, 3 (1951), 17–19.

H. B. Charlton, *Portrait of a University 1851–1951*, Manchester: Manchester University Press, 1951.

Clive H. Church, 'Constraints on the historian', *Studies in Higher Education*, 3, 2 (1978), 127–8.

M. J. Collie, 'Value and the teaching of literature', *Universities Quarterly*, 12 (1958), 181–8.

John Churton Collins, *The Study of English Literature: A Plea for its Recognition and Organisation at the Universities*, London: Macmillan, 1891.

Robert Colls and Philip Dodd, 'Representing the nation – British documentary film 1930–45', *Screen*, 26, 1 (1985), 21–33.

Robert Colls and Philip Dodd, eds, *Englishness: Politics and Culture 1880–1920*, Beckenham: Croom Helm, 1986.

Raymond Cowell, *The Critical Enterprise: English Studies in Higher Education*, London: Allen & Unwin, 1975.

C. B. Cox and A. E. Dyson, 'Word in the desert', *Critical Quarterly*, 10, 1/2 (1968), 1–7.

——*Fight for Education: A Black Paper*, London: Critical Quarterly Society, 1969.

—— *Black Paper Two: The Crisis in Education*, London: Critical Quarterly Society, 1970.

—— *Black Paper Three: Goodbye Mr. Short*, London: Critical Quarterly Society, 1970.

C. B. Cox and Rhodes Boyson, eds, *Black Paper 1975: The Fight for Education*, London: Dent, 1975.

—— *Black Paper 1977*, London: Temple Smith, 1977.

David Craig and Margot Heineman, eds, *Experiments in English Teaching*, London: Edward Arnold, 1976.

William W. Craik, *The Central Labour College, 1909–1929*, London: Lawrence & Wishart, 1964.

David Daiches, 'The place of English Studies in the Sussex scheme' in Daiches, ed., *The Idea of a New University*, London: Andre Deutsch, 1964.

David Daiches, ed., *The Idea of a New University: An Experiment in Sussex*, London: Andre Deutsch, 1964.

Mirian E. David, *The State, the Family and Education*, London: Routledge & Kegan Paul, 1980.

Tony Davies, 'Education, ideology and literature', *Red Letters*, 7 (1978), 4–15.

—— 'Common sense and critical practice: teaching literature' in Peter Widdowson, ed., *Re-Reading English*, London: Methuen, 1982.

—— 'Damning the tides: the new English and the reviewers', in M. Green, ed., *English and Cultural Studies: Broadening the Context*, London: John Murray, 1987.

Jacques Donzelot, *The Policing of Families*, London: Hutchinson, 1979.

Brian Doyle, 'Fictions and ideology 1920–1940', unpublished dissertation, Thames Polytechnic, 1978.

—— 'Against the tyranny of the past', *Red Letters*, 10 (n.d. [1980]), 23–33.

—— 'Some uses of English: Denys Thompson and the development of English in secondary schools', CCCS Stencilled Paper No. SP64, University of Birmingham, 1981.

—— 'The hidden history of English studies', in Peter Widdowson, ed., *Re-Reading English*, London: Methuen, 1982.

A. Durant, *Conditions of Music*, London: Macmillan, 1984.

Carol Dyhouse, 'Social Darwinistic ideas and the development of women's education in England, 1880–1920', *History of Education*, 5, 1 (1976), 41–58.

A. E. Dyson, 'Literature – in the younger universities', *Critical Quarterly*, 1, ii (1959), 116–23.

Terry Eagleton, 'The Cambridge Crisis', *Time Out*, 6 February 1981, 5.

—— *Literary Theory*, Oxford: Basil Blackwell, 1983.

Michael Eaton, 'Lie back and think of England', in Eileen Phillips, ed., *The Left and the Erotic*, London: Lawrence & Wishart, 1983.

English Association, *Bulletin*, 1–50 (1907–1924), and other selected Bulletins and Pamphlets.

English Studies Group, 'Recent developments in English Studies at the Centre', in Stuart Hall, et al., eds, *Culture, Media, Language: Working Papers in Cultural Studies 1972–79*, London: Hutchinson and CCCS, 1979.

W. D. Emrys Evans, 'Survey of the surveys', *Critical Survey*, 3, 3 (1967), 184–8.

Colin Falck, 'Liberal studies', *TLS*, 25 July 1968, 797–8.

John Fekete, *The Critical Twilight: Explorations in the Ideology of Anglo-American Literary Theory form Eliot to McLuhan*, London: Routledge & Kegan Paul, 1978.

C. H. Firth, *The School of English Language and Literature: A Contribution to the History of Oxford Studies*, Oxford: Basil Blackwell, 1909.

Boris Ford, ed., *The New Pelican Guide to English Literature*, 8 vols, Harmondsworth: Penguin, 1983.

Michel Foucault, *The Archaeology of Knowledge*, London: Tavistock, 1974.

—— *The History of Sexuality*, Harmondsworth: Allen Lane, 1979.

—— *Power/Knowledge: Selected Interviews and Other Writings 1972–1977*, Brighton: Harvester, 1980.

Eric Frykman, *W. F. Aytoun; Pioneer Professor of English*, Gothenburg Studies in English, vol. 17, n.d.

Helen Gardner, 'The academic study of English literature', *Critical Quarterly*, 1, ii (1959), 106–15.

K. W. S. Garwood, 'The development of the teaching of English 1830–1920', unpublished thesis, University of Wales, 1954.

P. Gilroy, *There Ain't No Black in the Union Jack*, London: Hutchinson, 1987.

G. S. Gordon, 'The discipline of letters', Oxford Inaugural Lecture, 1923, in G. S. Gordon, *The Discipline of Letters*, Oxford: Clarendon Press, 1946.

—— *The Discipline of Letters*, Oxford: Clarendon Press, 1946.

Colin Gordon, *The Foundation of the University of Salford*, Altringham: Sherratt, 1975.

Ian A. Gordon, *The Teaching of English: A Study in Secondary Education*, Christchurch: New Zealand Council for Educational Research, 1947.

M. Green, ed., *English and Cultural Studies: Broadening the Context*, London: John Murray, 1987.

John Gross, *The Rise and Fall of the Man of Letters: Aspects of English Literary Life since 1800*, Harmondsworth: Penguin, 1973.

Guardian, 'Dons in bitter row over English literary policy', 16 January 1981, 1, 32.

——'Critical day for critics' critics', 4 February 1981, 1–2.

——'Oxford joins the battle of the dons', 7 February 1981, 2.

——'Dons may testify on English row', 18 February 1981, 2.

——'New post offer to don in English dispute', 30 May 1981, 1.

——'The revenge of structuralism's apostle', 10 October 1981, 5.

Stuart Hall, Dorothy Hobson, Andrew Lowe, and Paul Willis, eds, *Culture, Media, Language: Working Papers in Cultural Studies 1972–79*, London: Hutchinson and CCCS, 1979.

Barbara Hardy, 'The teaching of literature in the university', *English in Education*, Spring 1973, 26–38.

J. F. C. Harrison, *Learning and Living 1790–1960: A Study in the History of the English Adult Education Movement*, London: Routledge & Kegan Paul, 1961.

T. R. Henn, 'The shape of English teaching', in Peter Bander, ed., *Looking Forward to the Seventies*, London: Colin Smythe, 1968.

J. Hearn, *The Gender of Oppression*, Brighton: Wheatsheaf, 1987.

J. Hearn and W. Parkin, *'Sex' at 'Work': The Power and Paradox of Organisation Sexuality*, Brighton: Wheatsheaf, 1987.

E. J. Hobsbawm, *Industry and Empire*, Harmondsworth: Penguin, 1969.

J. T. Hodgson, 'Changes in English teaching: institutionalisation, transmission and ideology', unpublished thesis, University of London, 1974.

Richard Hoggart, 'English in extra-mural education', *Universities Quarterly*, 5, 3 (1951), 251–9.

——*The Uses of Literacy: Aspects of Working-Class Life with Special Reference to Publications and Entertainments* (1957), Harmondsworth: Penguin, 1962.

——'Why I value literature', in Steiner et al., *The Critical Moment*, London: Faber, 1964.

——'The literary imagination and the study of society', CCCS Occasional Paper no. 3, University of Birmingham, 1967.

——'Contemporary cultural studies: an approach to the study of literature and society', CCCS Occasional Paper no. 6, University of Birmingham, 1969.

Graham Hough, 'Crisis in literary education', in J. H. Plumb, ed., *Crisis in the Humanities*, Harmondsworth: Penguin, 1964.

——'The function of imagination', in Steiner et al., *The Critical Moment*, London: Faber, 1964.

——'Criticism as a humanist discipline', in Malcolm Bradbury and David Palmer, eds, *Contemporary Criticism*, London: Edward Arnold, 1970.

——'The turn of the native', *TLS*, 4 March 1983, 217.

T. E. B. Howarth, *Cambridge Between the Wars*, London: Collins, 1978.

Fred Inglis, *The Englishness of English Teaching*, London: Longman, 1969.

—— 'Attention to education: Leavis and the Leavisites', *Universities Quarterly*, 30, 1 (1975), 94–106.

K. S. Inglis, *Churches and the Working Classes in Victorian England*, London: Routledge & Kegan Paul, 1963.

D. G. James, 'The teaching of English in universities', *Universities Quarterly*, 5, 3 (1951), 232–8 and 304.

Richard Johnson, 'Barrington Moore, Perry Anderson and English social development', *Cultural Studies*, 9 (1976), 7–28.

Terence J. Johnson, *Professions and Power*, London: Macmillan, 1972.

Gareth Stedman Jones, *Outcast London: A Study in the Relationship between Classes in Victorian Society*, Oxford: Clarendon Press, 1971.

Mervyn Jones, 'The Oxbridge malaise', *Guardian*, 14 February 1981, 9.

Hugh Kearney, 'University and society in historical perspective', in R. E. Bell and A. J. Youngson, eds, *Present and Future in Higher Education*, London: Tavistock, 1973.

Peter Keating, ed., *Into Unknown England*, London: Fontana, 1976.

Owen Kelly, *Community, Art and the State: Storming the Citadels*, London: Comedia, 1984.

The Kingman Committee, *Report of the Committee of Inquiry into the Teaching of English Language*, London: HMSO, 1988.

James Kinsley, *English Studies in the University*, inaugural lecture, Swansea: University College, 1954.

—— 'English Studies at Nottingham', *Critical Survey*, 1, 2 (1963), 118–22.

Ben Knights, *The Idea of the Clericy in the Nineteenth Century*, Cambridge: Cambridge University Press, 1978.

L. C. Knights, 'The university teaching of English and History: a plea for correlation', in *Explorations: Essays in Criticism Mainly on the Literature of the Seventeenth Century*, London: Chatto & Windus, 1946.

David Kynaston, *King Labour: The British Working Class 1850–1914*, London: Allen & Unwin, 1976.

F. R. Leavis, 'Two cultures? The significance of C. P. Snow', The Richmond Lecture, 1962, *Spectator*, 9 March 1962.

—— *Education and the University: A Sketch for an 'English School'* (1943), London: Chatto & Windus, 1965.

—— *English Literature in Our Time and the University: The Clark Lectures 1967*, London: Chatto & Windus, 1969.

—— *The Living Principle: English as a Discipline of Thought*, London: Chatto & Windus, 1975.

David Lodge, ed., *20th Century Literary Criticism*, London: Longman, 1972.

T. Lovell, *Consuming Fiction*, London: Verso, 1987.

F. L. Lucas, 'English literature', in Harold Wright, ed., *University Studies Cambridge 1933*, Cambridge: Ivor Nicholson & Watson, 1933.

John Lucas, ed., *Literature and Politics in the Nineteenth Century*, London: Methuen, 1971.

D. Lusted, 'English teaching and media education: culture and the curriculum', in M. Green, ed., *English and Cultural Studies: Broadening the Context*, London: John Murray, 1987.

Pierre Macherey and Etienne Balibar, 'Literature as an ideological form: some marxist propositions', *Oxford Literary Review*, 3, 1 (1978), 4–12.

Colin MacCabe, 'The sunset of the British Empire', *Guardian*, 28 February 1983, 9.

J. S. Maclure, *Educational Documents, England and Wales 1816–1967*, Oxford: Oxford University Press, 1968.

Robert G. MacPherson, *The Theory of Higher Education in Nineteenth-Century England*, Athens, Georgia: University of Georgia Press, 1959.

Arthur Marwick, *Britain in a Century of Total War*, Harmondsworth: Penguin, 1970.

Margaret Mathieson, *The Preachers of Culture: A Study of English and its Teachers*, London: Allen & Unwin, 1975.

Keith Middlemas, *Politics in Industrial Society: The Experience of the British System since 1911*, London: Andre Deutsch, 1979.

Frank Mort, 'A strategy for English: cultural politics and English Studies', *Cencrastus*, 16 (1984), 24–7.

James Mountford, *Keele: An Historical Critique*, London: Routledge & Kegan Paul, 1972.

Francis Mulhern, *The Moment of 'Scrutiny'*, London: New Left Books, 1979.

—— 'The Cambridge affair', *Marxism Today*, 25, 3 (1981), 27–8.

—— 'Intelligentsia regroups to fight the British crisis', *THES*, 22 May 1981, 11–12.

W. R. Mullins, 'A study of significant changes in the theory of the teaching of English to older pupils in Elementary and Secondary Modern Schools, 1860–1960', unpublished thesis, University of Leicester, 1968.

P. W. Musgrave, ed., *Sociology, History, and Education*, London: Methuen, 1972.

Newbolt Report, *The Teaching of English in England: Being the Report of the Departmental Committee Appointed by the President of the Board of Education to Inquire into the Position of English in the Education System of England*, London: HMSO, 1921.

J. M. Newton, 'English Literature at the university: a historical enquiry', unpublished thesis, Clare College, Cambridge, 1963.

E. R. Norman, *Church and Society in England 1770–1970*, Oxford: Clarendon Press, 1976.

Observer, 'Structuralists' full house', 1 February 1981, 2.

Raymond O'Malley, 'Charisma?', in Denys Thompson, ed., *The Leavises: Recollections and Impressions*, Cambridge: Cambridge University Press, 1984.

Walter J. Ong, *Orality and Literacy: The Technologising of the World*, London: Methuen, 1982.

George Orwell, 'Politics and the English language' (1946), in *Inside the Whale and Other Essays*, Harmondsworth: Penguin, 1972.

Elizabeth Owen and John Oakley, '"English" and the Council for National Academic Awards', in Peter Widdowson, ed., *Re-Reading English*, London: Methuen, 1982.

K. Owusu, *The Struggle for Black Arts in Britain*, London: Comedia, 1985.

Michael Paffard, *Thinking About English*, London: Ward Lock, 1978.

D. J. Palmer, *The Rise of English Studies: An Account of the Study of English Language and Literature from its Origins to the Making of the Oxford English School*, Oxford: Oxford University Press, 1965.

Christopher J. W. Parker, 'The development of History courses in British universities 1850–1975', unpublished thesis, Exeter University, 1976.

—— 'Academic history: paradigms and dialectic', *Literature and History*, 5, 2 (1979), 165–82.

Patrick Parrinder, 'Sermons, pseudo-science and critical discourse: some reflections on the aims and methods of contemporary English', *Studies in Higher Education*, 4, 1 (1979), 3–13.

Nicholas M. Pearson, *The State and Visual Arts: A Discussion of State Intervention in the Visual Arts in Britain 1760–1981*, Milton Keynes: Open University Press, 1982.

Barry Phillips, 'The politics of literacy: starting points', *The Radical Teacher*, 8 (1978), 1–4.

Eileen Phillips, ed., *The Left and the Erotic*, London: Lawrence & Wishart, 1983.

V. de Sola Pinto, 'Notes on the School of English Studies in the University of Nottingham', *Universities Quarterly*, 5, 3 (1951), 225–31.

J. H. Plumb, ed., *Crisis in the Humanities*, Harmondsworth: Penguin, 1964.

Stephen Potter, *The Muse in Chains: A Study in Education*, London: Jonathan Cape, 1937.

Arthur Quiller-Couch, *On the Art of Writing* (1916), Cambridge: Cambridge University Press, 1928.

R. Quirk and A. H. Smith (eds), *The Teaching of English*, London: Secker & Warburg, 1959.

Louis Arnaud Reid, 'The nature and justification of an "Arts" education', *Universities Quarterly*, 3, 1 (1948), 497–504.

Review of English Studies, vols I to XVI (1925–40), and selected subsequent issues.

Melvin Richter, *The Politics of Conscience: T. H. Green and his Age*, London: Weidenfeld & Nicholson, 1964.

Robbins Report, *Higher Education*, London: HMSO, 1963.

W. W. Robson, 'The future of English Studies', *TLS*, 25 July 1968, 773–4.

Allan Rodway and Mark Roberts, 'English in the University II: "practical criticism" in principle and practice', *Essays in Criticism*, X, 1 (1960), 1–17.

Pat Rogers, *The Courage to be Literary*, Winchester: King Alfred's College, 1979.

Nikolas Rose, 'The psychological complex: mental measurement and social administration', *Ideology and Consciousness*, 5 (1979), 5–68.

Sheldon Rothblatt, *Tradition and Change in English Liberal Education: An Essay in History and Culture*, London: Faber, 1976.

Fredrick Rudolph, *Curriculum: a History of the American Undergraduate Course of Study since 1636*, San Francisco, Calif.: Jossey-Bass, 1977.

Edward Said, 'Opponents, audiences, constituencies and community', in Hal Foster, ed., *Postmodern Culture*, London: Pluto Press, 1985.

George Sampson, *English for the English: A Chapter on National Education*, Cambridge: Cambridge University Press, 1921, reprinted 1926.

Michael Sanderson, ed., *The Universities in the Nineteenth Century*, London: Routledge & Kegan Paul, 1975.

J. W. Saunders, *The Profession of English Letters*, London: Routledge & Kegan Paul, 1964.

Hilda Schiff, ed., *Contemporary Approaches to English Studies*, London: Heinemann, 1977.

G. R. Searle, *The Quest for National Efficiency: A Study in British Politics and British Political Thought 1899–1914*, Oxford: Basil Blackwell, 1971.

David Shayer, *The Teaching of English in Schools 1900–70*, London: Routledge & Kegan Paul, 1972.

A. N. Shimmin, *The University of Leeds: The First Half Century*, Cambridge: Cambridge University Press, 1954.

Brian Simon, *Education and the Labour Movement 1870–1920*, London: Lawrence & Wishart, 1965.

D. Sless, *In Search of Semiotics*, Beckenham: Croom Helm, 1986.

Albert E. Sloman, *A University in the Making*, 1963 Reith Lectures, London: BBC, 1964.

Nowell Smith, *The Origins and History of the Association*, Chairman's Address, London: English Association, 1942.

Carole Snee, 'Period studies and the place of criticism', in Peter Widdowson, ed., *Re-Reading English*, London: Methuen, 1982.

C. P. Snow, *The Two Cultures and the Scientific Revolution*, The Rede Lecture, 1959, Cambridge: Cambridge University Press, 1959.

H. S. Solly, *The Life of Henry Morley, LL.D.*, London: Edward Arnold, 1898.

John Sparrow, *Mark Pattison and the Idea of a University*, The Clark Lectures 1965, Cambridge: Cambridge University Press, 1967.

George Steiner, 'Humane literacy' in George Steiner et al., *The Critical Moment*, London: Faber, 1964.

George Steiner, 'Why English?' in Hilda Schiff, ed., *Contemporary Approaches to English Studies*, London: Heinemann, 1977.

G. Steiner, R. Hoggart, and G. Hough (eds), *The Critical Moment*, London: Faber, 1964.

Brian V. Street, *Literacy in Theory and Practice*, Cambridge: Cambridge University Press, 1985.

E. H. Tawney, 'Social history and literature' (1949), in *The Radical Tradition*, London: Allen & Unwin, 1964.

A. J. P. Taylor, *English History 1914–1945*, Oxford: Clarendon Press, 1965.

Denys Thompson, ed., *The Leavises: Recollections and Impressions*, Cambridge: Cambridge University Press, 1984.

THES, 'Cambridge scholars wage literal warfare', 23 January 1981, 3.
—— 'MacCabe gets a fellowship', 20 February 1981, 3.
—— 'New post for MacCabe', 5 June 1981, 2.
—— 'Strathclyde structure suits MacCabe', 26 June 1981, 3.

E. M. W. Tillyard, *The Muse Unchained: An Intimate Account of the Revolution in English Studies at Cambridge*, Cambridge: Bowes & Bowes, 1958.

TLS, 'Mincing words' (editorial), 25 July 1968, 767.
—— A series of reports on 'The present state of English Studies at some universities': nine weekly articles by a 'Special Correspondent', 11 February–14 April 1972.

R. C. Townsend, 'The idea of an English School: Cambridge English', *Critical Survey*, 3, iii (1967), 129–43.

University Grants Committee, *Statistics of Education*, vol. 6, *Universities*, London: HMSO, 1971.

William Walsh, 'A level look', *TLS*, 25 July 1968, 777–8.

Garry Watson, *The Leavises, the 'Social' and the Left*, Swansea: Brynmill, 1977.

George Watson, *The Literary Critics. A Study of English Descriptive Criticism*, Harmondsworth: Penguin, 1964.

Rene Wellek and Austin Warren, *Theory of Literature*, Harmondsworth: Penguin, 1976.

Peter Widdowson, 'Literature in society', in David Craig and Margot Heineman, eds, *Experiments in English Teaching*, London: Edward Arnold, 1976.

—— '"Literary value" and the reconstruction of criticism', *Literature and History*, 6, 2 (1980), 138–50.

Peter Widdowson, ed., *Re-Reading English: Essays on Literature and Criticism in Higher Education*, London: Methuen, 1982.

R. H. Wilkinson, 'The gentleman ideal and the maintenance of a political elite', in P. W. Musgrave, ed., *Sociology, History, and Education*, London: Methuen, 1972.

Basil Willey, *The Seventeenth Century Background*, Harmondsworth: Penguin, 1962.

—— *The Eighteenth Century Background*, Harmondsworth: Penguin, 1962.

—— *Cambridge and Other Memories 1920–53*, London: Chatto & Windus, 1968.

Raymond Williams, *Culture and Society 1780–1950*, London: Chatto & Windus, 1958.

—— *Communications*, Harmondsworth: Penguin, 1962.

—— *Keywords: A Vocabulary of Culture and Society*, London: Fontana, 1976.

—— 'Literature in society', in Hilda Schiff, ed., *Contemporary Approaches to English Studies*, London: Heinemann, 1977.

—— *Politics and Letters*, London: New Left Books, 1979.

—— 'The Bloomsbury fraction', in *Problems in Materialism and Culture*, London: Verso, 1980.

—— 'Marxism, structuralism and literary analysis', *New Left Review*, 129 (1981), 51–66.

—— *Culture*, London: Fontana, 1981.

J. Dover Wilson, *Milestones on the Dover Road*, London: Faber, 1969.

A. Wood, 'To provide for the nation', *Royal Society of Arts News*, 8, Summer 1985, 7.

A. C. Wood, *A History of University College, Nottingham 1881–1948*, Oxford: Basil Blackwell, 1953.

Harold Wright, ed., *University Studies Cambridge 1933*, Cambridge: Ivor Nicholson & Watson, 1933.

Iain Wright, 'On the social responsibility of literature', *THES*, 12 November 1976, 17.

Index